LOST IN HAWAII
OUR 17-YEAR FAMILY VACATION

LOST IN HAWAII
OUR 17-YEAR FAMILY VACATION

ANDY STENNETT

Published by

Ohana Island Service

Various names in this memoir have been anonymized. Some dialogues are representations of conversations had and sentiments felt during our experiences.

Disclaimer: Although our family enjoyed the activities described in this book, we do not recommend any or all of them to any particular family or individual. Some involve risks of serious injury or death, and readers are cautioned to consider the risks that they are willing to undertake on behalf of themselves or their families. We have merely described our own experiences, and we accept no responsibility or liability for any activities anyone undertakes or participates in as a result of reading this book.

Dedicated to Sharon, our children, Mother, all parents
and grandparents, Hawaii, and family adventure.

Special thanks to Sarah Hale, Braiden Lindstrom,
Karen Edwards, Douglas Higham Sr., Richard Mauldin,
Kent Minson, and Jana Eliason.

Map of the Jungle Patch illustrated by Mos Stennett

To the BEACH

MONKEYPOD TREE

BUFFALO GRASS REALMS

The LANE

golf balls

KING RUBBER TREE

GRAPEFRUIT TREE

LOST WOODS

The JUNGLE PATCH
- and -
Surrounding Areas

Contents

Introduction xi

CHAPTER ONE
Trench Warfare and
Paris Dial-Up 1

CHAPTER TWO
First Impressions and Digs 12

CHAPTER THREE
Kauai Study Abroad:
The Land 24

CHAPTER FOUR
Kauai Study Abroad:
The People and Culture 32

CHAPTER FIVE
The Jungle House 44

CHAPTER SIX
The Jungle Patch 55

CHAPTER SEVEN
Raising Jungle Patch Kids 66

CHAPTER EIGHT
Education in the
Jungle Patch 78

CHAPTER NINE
Jungle Patch Adventures—Unplugged   92

CHAPTER TEN
Kauai Aesop's Fables:
The Jungle Cats   101

CHAPTER ELEVEN
Kauai Adventure:
The Jungle Patch Guide   108

CHAPTER TWELVE
The Pest-War Misadventures   128

CHAPTER THIRTEEN
How We Made a Living: Rooster Humor
and Golf Balls   137

CHAPTER FOURTEEN
The Adventure of
Making a Difference   151

SUMMARY
An Empty Jungle
Patch Nest   170

FINAL THOUGHTS
A Jungle Patch Husband   174

Introduction

Another Kauai sunset is soaking our Haden mango tree with hushed golden light. I am perched somewhat precariously on one of the tree's branches, plucking its plump, ruddy fruits. Below me on the jungle floor is my ten-year-old daughter waiting anxiously to catch the mangoes as I toss them down. As she skips to the nearby porch to add them to our harvest, I fade into a moment of reflection. How on earth did I wind up on this faraway island, living a life such as this?

I am driven to wander and discover. Curious cultures call to me. Tranquil landscapes—especially ones wreathed in tropical greens and sunlit ocean blues—summon me to pack a bag and try a sample residence. Fueling my urge to wander is a genetic gift/curse—an inner whirlwind of nonstop physical energy. To win a good night's sleep, I must power down the pesky whirlwind through an after-work fray of yard work, or pedalling, or swimming, or all of them. Complicating this fusion of drives, I am a husband and a father of six. My poor wife and kids! Since family time is my passion, they have often wound up as wearied partners in yet another of my energy-burning escapades. Yes, bonding in our family has been unmapped and bumpy at times—but, also, unforgettable.

My nomadism first showed up when I was a boy toiling in the flat, fenced farmlands surrounding my home in Eden,

Idaho. I frequently gazed at the distant snow-capped Sun Valley mountains and daydreamed of jaunts beyond. Suddenly, I had hurdled the cattle fence and transformed into an intrepid explorer rafting in the cool whitewater of the Salmon River! But then, an ill-mannered clank of machinery jolted me back to reality. "Argh, still a sweating farm boy," I grumbled, as I stacked another bale of hay.

I was smitten with castaway stories like *The Swiss Family Robinson* because they captured the blast of the unknown that I yearned for. Little did I know that someday my nomadism and surplus energy would propel me as a grown man on a journey that mirrored these stories. It would lead me and my family beyond the Sun Valley mountains to a faraway island where we would live an adventure tale of our own.

Of course, in our tale there were differences. Our setting was not an uncharted island—it was Kauai, Hawaii, near Kalapaki Beach, in a place called the Jungle Patch. There weren't any pirates or tigers to battle. The worst it got was some heated arguments with jungle swine that provoked us from time to time. Neither was there a mushy love triangle. It was just the eight of us loving and taking care of each other.

In our story, there was no treehouse either. We dwelt in a slanting house covered by a rusting metal roof and shaded by a jagged halo of Java plum and mango trees. Lastly, we were not shipwrecked—just a bit self-marooned when we fell under Hawaii's charms on a vacation and forgot to go home.

There in the Jungle Patch, while the world bustled around us, we lived chapter upon chapter of a seventeen-year island odyssey. Was it chancy to do such a thing? Yes—but my wife and I are glad we did it. By following a pathway of serendipity, our family uncovered a treasure of playful adventures, misadventures, aha moments, and heartwarming friends as we merged with incredible Hawaii. And now our tale has become the glue of an understanding that binds us together. With the children raised and spread from Virginia to Japan, we communicate through our smartphones. But it is through our jungle house memories that we understand one another.

For all its rosiness, however, our bonding did not come without a price. In all gains in life, there are unintended losses. In following my gypsyness, I transformed my energy into living daydreams; but in doing so, I created conflict. I knew that my wife hungered for a permanent nest, and my children wanted familiarity, friends, and stability. I struggled to fathom an endgame: when would I finally stop wandering and allow my family to have these gifts they so deserved?

Things do have a way of working themselves out. My story is about the unlikely resolution between a father's restlessness and his family responsibilities. May it spark or re-spark a gentle fever of restlessness in fathers, mothers, and families everywhere, just enough to write their own adventure tales. May those tales—whether written in their own backyard or on a distant island—bind them together forever.

CHAPTER ONE

Trench Warfare and Paris Dial-Up

It is January 1998. I am engulfed in trench warfare in our mountain village of St. Charles, Idaho. The triple-axis foe of waist-deep snow, gray skies, and subzero temps are clobbering my morale. Each morning, I mummify myself in wooly wraps and trudge outside the house to fight. On my ATV snowplow steed, I charge full throttle at a bank of snow and rip open a walking trench from the house to the vehicle yard. From there, I gouge out a vehicle trench to the county road. At dusk, after a long day's work, I plow away the minions of drifting snow invading my gains. I glance longingly at the house's brightly-lit windows. Inside, a warm reunion with Sharon and the kids awaits. But first, I must plug in the block heaters of the pickup and Suburban in the hopes they will start in the morning. "Tomorrow, I will mummify, plow, plow, plow . . . to whom do I send the white flag?" I chuckle into the frozen night.

It wasn't that my wife, Sharon, and I didn't love living in St. Charles, nestled in Idaho's lonesome Bear Lake Valley. Except for the mile-high winters, it was a family paradise. In our cozy home, I roughhoused with the kids, dozed through chick flicks, and got extra hugs by fixing broken toys and leaky faucets. Our brood of kids safely roamed to the lone town market, while legendary raspberries flourished in the cool summer air. Meeting our daily gaze was a 360-degree pan-orama of mountains and forests, accented with autumn red, spring green, winter white, and summer bronze. In nearby Bloomington Canyon, there was a mountain-top, crystal-clear lake. On the lakeshore, dangling from the limb of a lofty ever-green, was a Tom Sawyer rope swing—exactly the brand of storybook fun this dad wanted to offer his kids.

I had pledged to never leave this alpine oasis. Bear Lake was the reward of a thirsting pilgrimage to regain my coun-try-boy roots, stolen away by the traditional fast lane of getting ahead. It all started when I plodded off to college, forsaking my hayseed life on the sagebrush plains of Eden (population 365) and my happy wanderings into the Sun Valley moun-tains. Next, came a goodwill stint in Thailand, marriage to Sharon (a spunky humanitarian whom I met in Thailand), a marketing job in California, more schooling, and finally employment with the federal government in Washington, D.C. And though my career as an analyst was intriguing and promising, D.C. had an unacceptably high concrete-to-soil ratio for this country lad.

Longing for open space, I counseled with Sharon, gave my notice at work, loaded up our three little sons, and migrated to urban zip codes in the West. After cobbling together a nest egg by turning some fixer-upper real estate (and after gaining three more children), I reached the end of my pilgrimage when we bought a sixty-acre hay farm near Bear Lake and planted our-selves in a 1930s bungalow in St. Charles.

But this planting was more than the end of a pilgrimage. It was a personal line drawn in the sand; it was where I would lay my wanderlust to rest. When I was young, my father chased his own restless dreams, bouncing our family from Illinois to Minnesota, to South Dakota, to Colorado, and finally to many towns in Idaho. My older three siblings and I knew well the whiplash of changing schools and making new friends again and again.

Now I had unwittingly fallen into the same rut. I had found it "necessary" to move our family ten or more times within four different states in fourteen years of marriage. Poor Sharon. She had been happily anchored in the same house from birth to graduating from nursing school. One of her worst childhood fears was the thought of leaving her comfortable home and neighborhood. Fast forward to life with me. Although she had adopted a cheerful, bloom-where-you're-planted attitude, I knew that our many migrations while she birthed and nurtured our children were getting old.

After unloading her piano (which she loved to play) in our St. Charles house, I revealed my thank-offering for her support, "Honey, the kids will never have to change schools again, and I am going to build you an airy log home on our sixty-acres." She was relieved! My life's path was now set. I would bury my wandering ways and channel my energy into raising our young 'uns in the country. I, too, was relieved—but for a different reason: I would have to move her elephantine piano just one last time!

A SEASON IN THE SUN

Despite my honest intent to stay put, when Bear Lake's Arctic thermometer plummeted, a nomad's daydream came tempting. I titled it "A Season in the Sun." When the snow trenches grew cheerless, I pushed "play" and slipped into its anesthetic reverie. There before me was a secluded tropical island beneath a brilliant blue sky. On a palm-lined beach warmed by the kiss of a lemon-yellow sun, I saw Sharon and the kids romping. Suddenly, there was a wild man on that beach flirting with her and roughhousing with the kids—me!

Abetting my daydream was the phone company down the road in Paris. (No joke, Idaho has a Paris, sans Louvre and Eiffel grandeur.) It offered cutting-edge dial-up internet that gave "instant" access to scenes of tropical destinations. I was staring at sanguine greenery from islands of the Pacific on my computer screen and cajoling Sharon, "Honey, what do you think about American Samoa? Whoa, look at Fiji." But out of the corner of my eye, I saw an opposite reality. Snow trench minions had morphed their attack into a vertical pincer movement to capture me. Day-melt icicles from the eaves were marching steadily downward to meet the snow piling up past the window sills. I would soon be their prisoner. Recovering gypsy or not, I announced, "Dear, we're doin' a season in the sun for six months. Let's have the kids ready to go by daybreak!"

Isaac and Eric in the snow trenches

MY DAYDREAM SPUTTERS TO LIFE

At first, I'm fairly certain she patiently played along as we researched toasty island retreats. But realizing this was more than a passing "Andy whim," she proactively proposed Kauai, Hawaii. It was remote and warm—but it wasn't a deserted island with only coconuts and fish to eat. A portal of opportunity blinked open when Sharon (who had put her nursing career in storage to mother our brood) applied to the Kauai County hospital for an on-call position in labor and delivery.

Over the phone a chilled-out recruiter said, "We'd love to have you." And pitching the fringe benefits, the recruiter added, "Just think of all the money you'll save not buying snow tires!"

Though the astonishing good news about snow tires was encouraging, we were still a little worried about Hawaii's apocalypse of expense. (Six bucks for a gallon of milk?!) But with the promise of a cash flow from Sharon's nursing, and borrowing from our savings, we concluded that six months was doable. We saw a green light and stepped on the gas.

The Kauai portal widened when a resourceful travel agent in Logan, Utah called me back and reported, "Looks like I can get you one-way tickets to Kauai for $192 a piece." With visions of palm-lined beaches dancing in my head, I did some mental math: 8 x $192 = $1,600 (close enough). Hmm . . . 1,600 bucks for therapeutic sunshine, flip-flops and surf-shorts dress code, a "study abroad" for the kids, and family memories that would last a lifetime?

Snapping out of my tropical trance, I blurted out, "Here is my card number. Sign us up." Bam! It was settled. We would put our sentimentals and better belongings in our 20-foot construction trailer, sell or donate our other stuff (what a cleanse), and board a plane on December 2, 1998 bound for Kauai.

Of course, there was a question that all sensible people would ask: where would we house our octagon troop when we got there? Although we're not backpacker-frugal, we didn't want to blow wads of money on pillow space. But hey, it was

Hawaii; expensive and Hawaii are synonymous. Using trusty Paris dial-up, we reserved a modest east-shore vacation rental in Kapaa Town for a week. This would give us a window to sniff around for something affordable and more long-term.

On paper the Kauai plan looked simple enough, but it was about to meet its field test: transporting half a dozen kids (ages two through thirteen) and all their gear across an ocean. We were pretty lucky as parents. Our kids mostly favored Sharon's exceptionally easy-going temperament and would likely make the trip without much drama.

CAST OF CHARACTERS

I was confident Isaac, our oldest, would be a good team captain. He aptly fit the birth-order profile of a first child—anxious to please and achieve. I also knew fun-loving Eric would fall in line, although he aptly fit the profile of a second child who sometimes liked to test his boundaries. Middle-child Lucas was mellow and got his attention by creating subtle hilarity. Whenever I tucked him into bed, he often stalled by posing complex questions like, "Dad, how does electricity work?" Aaron, also sandwiched in the middle, was equally persuadable. Of all the kids, he was the most excited about the upcoming airplane rides because he had a passion for big machines. Cuddly Katherine would be calm as long as she had her silky pink blanket to stroke while she sucked her thumb.

And then there was Jordan. Jordan, Jordan! I wouldn't have wagered a single penny during his toddler years that he would someday mature into a sweet, level-headed young man. His grandmother (who loved him dearly) often said, "That child is a holy terror." He launched into frequent tantrums that lasted until he ran out of tears or lung power. The

In St. Charles prior to departure (left to right) Sharon, Jordan, Andy, Eric, Isaac, Lucas, Katherine, Aaron

one remedy that sometimes worked was to video his fit and instantly replay it on the camcorder display to summon him back to reality. I worried about a meltdown somewhere over the ocean at 36,000 feet and not being able to calm him down.

AN UNINTENDED COMEDY SKIT

Luckily, a Jordan huff never occurred, but there were some awkward moments along the way. Our Idaho-to-Kauai journey could best be summarized as a bumbling comedy skit.

Act One: BAFFLED, as in the baffled looks on the faces of fellow fliers inspecting our troop thronging airport foyers with nine pontoon-sized duffel bags in tow. "Are all these yours?" a stranger asked.

"Yes, every last bag . . . and all the kids, too," I replied, projecting a smiling public composure. We enacted a mandatory headcount at each connection and boarding gate (yes, we had watched *that* movie) and then wedged ourselves into yet another queue of passengers waiting to board. Miraculously, we eventually found ourselves seated (hopefully) on the right plane headed for Hawaii.

Act Two: TRAVESTY. Anxiously staring out our windows at the LAX tarmac, the loudspeaker crackled to life, "Ladies and gentlemen this is the captain speaking. We're sorry to report that the food elevator door is jammed, and it will be necessary to deplane until repairs are completed. Thank you for your patience." Sharon and I exchanged nervous glances. Of all the times for the silly food elevator door to jam, this had to be the one? There were signs of restlessness (mutiny) stirring in the ranks, not to mention the latent threat of a Jordan meltdown.

We scrambled into action. During our six-hour delay we invoked every magic trick in the book to absorb the kids' (and Dad's) energy. One was the powerful spell of food. Thankfully, the airline provided vouchers which we used to make a small capital investment in Burger King LAX: $75 worth of edibles. This "Whopper" of an order produced more bemused looks from onlookers, but it did its job. Many bags of burgers, fries, and apple pies later, we were finally reboarding.

Act Three: UNSCHEDULED NIGHT, as in we missed our connecting flight to Kauai, causing an unplanned night in Honolulu. The airline put us up in a nearby hotel. It was here that Act Four, MERCIFULLY OVER, played out. Sitting in the hotel restaurant waiting for our food, Sharon looked me in the eye and rhetorically mumbled, "Is this what it feels like to be a zombie?" I nodded incoherently, and oddly, in sync with the thumping pulse of island Christmas rock and roll blaring from the adjacent lounge. I took note of the only other customer in the room, a well-dressed businessman at a nearby table staring hard at some fixed point on the wall.

Suddenly, little Katherine—who had had one plane ride too many—vomited across the table. Sharon jumped up to assist while Lucas and Aaron slunk under the table to conceal their identities. Our dining

The adventure begins!

neighbor, completely unfazed, continued to stare at his fixed point on the wall. (Had the drone of Christmas rock and roll hypnotized him?) It was one of those moments when a tired dad secretly wished he had a quantum fast-forward button to skip to the next scene in life. Thankfully, the comedy skit soon wound down to its curtain call. A waiter tidied up the mess, the two brothers emerged from hiding, and bellies were filled. We retreated to our rooms, collapsed onto our beds, and drifted away into the first night's sleep of our season in the sun.

KID COMMENTS

Isaac (13/30)[1]

I don't have the official stats on it, but I would estimate that until 1998, no one had ever moved directly from

---

[1] Arrived in Hawaii at age 13 / 30 years old when writing this comment.

St. Charles, Idaho to Lihue, Kauai. Stats like this, and the-other-side-of-the-world feel regarding my destination were probably what led my classmates to be amazed/confused as to why we were going to move across the Pacific Ocean. I didn't realize until later what an unconventional thing it was to move a family of eight to a remote tropical island. The memory collection machine running in my brain according to the criteria deemed important to a thirteen-year-old kid stored away the following:

1) My sister, Katherine, swallowing a doll battery at the eleventh hour before the trip.
2) Eating lots and lots of Whoppers in an airport.
3) Eating in a hotel dining room while staying over on Oahu for the night due to a missed flight.

Apparently a memory is only preserved in a teenage kid's mind if it's related to eating.

Eric (11/28)

I remember living in Bear Lake in a big house that was actually quite fun. I had some friends and was excited to be starting middle school (6th grade). My parents told us we were going to Hawaii. I don't remember being too shocked or taken back by it. I remember watching my dad watch a video on a '97 era PC about the Big Island. That video must have taken years to buffer and load in those dial-up days.

Aaron (7/24)

I don't remember exactly when it started, but I remember Mom and Dad talking about moving. I hadn't heard exactly where we'd be going, but I did hear things like American Samoa and Hawaii. At seven years of age I did not know much about life outside of Idaho, so I was worried I might have to learn another language if we moved to one of those places. My fears were soon put to rest as I realized Hawaii was very much a part of the United States and no additional language training would be necessary.

Katherine (4/21)

Apparently I caused a little bit of trouble but I don't remember any of it—not even barfing at the restaurant! But I do remember picking up that Barbie battery, sticking it in my mouth, and swallowing. I only wish I could remember my logic.

CHAPTER TWO

First Impressions and Digs

It is midmorning. I am standing on the covered balcony of the upstairs duplex in east-shore Lihue where we have settled for our sojourn. The clouds have burst, and the kids have fled the house to embrace the flying sheets of rain. On the concrete courtyard, I spy leaping Katherine and Sujong, her Korean neighbor friend. Their little arms are outstretched to greet the heaven-sent moisture. Jordan is madly pedaling his three-wheeler and appearing to hydroplane. Lucas and Aaron have become statues, heads tilted back, mouths wide open, drinking in the pure H_2O. Away in the southern distance is bold green Mt. Haupu, decked out in tiers of clouds. "I think I shall like living in Hawaii," I breathe to myself.

Yo! Everyone up. We're off to meet Kauai!" I rousted the jet-lagged crew from their soft hotel beds. Sharon and I then squeezed our octagon through a continental breakfast line, onto a shuttle, and on board an Aloha Airlines 737 bound for Kauai. The twenty-minute hop across the channel felt almost like cresting the hill of a roller coaster. Up we shot from Oahu and then, suddenly, we descended. We stared out the windows as the rugged misty island grew closer and closer.

"Whoa," exclaimed Isaac, "it has mountains."

"It's sooo green," added Lucas.

"Wow, it's totally like *Jurassic Park*," blurted out dinosaur-fan Eric.

The kids' excitement was validation enough for yesterday's comedy skit. We were now gazing at the home of one of the wettest spots on earth: Mt. Waialeale, which boasts an average annual rainfall of 430 inches per year. Her surrounding mountains and tablelands sloping out to sea are kept velvety green by the gift of her prolific rain cycles. So, this is where I shall animate my oceanic family daydream, I mused.

On the morning of our touchdown in Lihue, Mt. Waialeale was generous with her rain gifts. It was a bit ironic to kick off our season in the sun by dashing with our luggage to the rental van through squalls of rain. "Where are the blue skies and lemon-yellow sun?" I muttered. "At least it's warm and

December 5, 1998 arrival in Lihue

there's no snow to plow," I countered as I squished another duffel bag into the van.

Knowing Hawaii's islands have both a wet and a dry side, we jetted west for Kekaha on the dry side of the island. In this quiet rain-shadow town we switched our reservation from rainy Kapaa to a vacation rental located a block from the beach. The kids were fascinated by two especially exotic features of our new digs.

Big-eyed Eric exclaimed, "There's a coconut tree in the yard!" He shimmied up a few feet before bailing off.

From inside the house, there was a cry, "CABLE TV!!" All kid feet peeled into the living room. (We had never had cable.)

"Let's see what's on," Isaac said.

A minute later the kids were in a trance. While their eyes slowly glazed over, I wandered around the house. The tight craftsmanship mesmerized me. I imagined a scene of industrious island carpenters sawing, nailing, and framing the gorgeous tongue-and-groove, knotless-redwood planks into the walls surrounding me. Befuddling me, though, was the quirky plumbing. I puzzled out loud to Sharon, "Sheesh! The washing machine and water heater are plopped outside under the carport. In Bear Lake, that'd be a frozen, pipe-bursting disaster."

MEETING ISLAND MIGHT AND MISCHIEF

Anxious to get the party started on our first day, Lucas got full disclosure about the ocean's might and mischief. Dressed in street clothes, he zipped gleefully across the beach to the edge of the receding water and pivoted toward us. Just as he flashed an innocent grin and a double peace sign, a rogue wave crashed down on him, pummeling his little body in the surf. As the wave receded, he sprang to his feet in a fit of wild laughter—he had held his own against the mighty Pacific Ocean. This spirited moment became the more apropos kick-off to our season in the sun—and a lasting lesson to never turn one's back on the ocean.

On the next morning, while Sharon, the youngest two kids, and I were napping off jet lag, the oldest four ran off to the beach. There they met the might and mischief of the tropical sun. After several hours of digging in the sand, they returned. Their fair skin was glowing red.

"Oh my heavens," gasped Sharon, "I feel like the worst mom ever. I forgot to tell them to put sunscreen on!" After a dash to buy some aloe vera gel, we massaged it into their scorched skin.

"Mom, that hurts! Softer please," whimpered Aaron. The visual of lobster-red skin prompted a modification to our trip's title: "A Season in the Sun—with Sunscreen."

After a few days, the blue skies of my daydream had recuperated island-wide, and we migrated to a vacation cottage on the eastside in Kapaa. Directly across the street was a Swiss cheese-looking coral beach with tide pools for the kids to explore. They collected loose coral bits like they were pirate gold pieces. Inside the cottage, the air was moist and carried the pungent aroma of ocean. I was amazed at the toll the salt air had taken. The spindles connecting the door knobs on the vintage skeleton key handlesets were nearly eaten through. Pointing to an unprotected metal surface, I attempted a maintenance tutorial, "Guys, are you seeing this unchecked rust?"

Nobody looked up; they were again engulfed in the novel Hawaiian pastime of cable TV.

STICKER SHOCK AND SHAKA

At a nearby grocery store, Sharon bought a stockpile of food to feed our forever-famished kids. I was grateful for the food but, staring at the receipt in my trembling hand, sticker shock began to dampen the mood like ants at a picnic. The price of refueling the van with luxury tropical gasoline wasn't helping either. I knew stuff was going to cost 15-35% more than in Idaho, but multiplied by eight people for the next six months . . . argh!

Another damper was the bustling traffic. On rural Idaho roads, meeting a passing car or tractor was an event in which neighborly waves were exchanged. On Kauai, however, the roads were fairly congested with local commuters mingled with tourists zooming to luaus and beaches. The silver lining in this was a gesture of civility from most local drivers that renewed my faith in humanity. Even if they had the right of way, they would yield and motion for cars on the side streets to merge with or cross over lanes of traffic. Merging locals signaled *mahalo* or thanks by throwing out a *shaka* (a wave of the hand with only the thumb and pinky extended). The kindness was contagious. It wasn't long before I began to throw out novice shakas of my own to say, "*Mahalo,* Mr. Polite Driver! Have a nice day!"

Shunning these minor negatives, and seeing there was not a snow trench in sight, I resolved to romp with the kids and Sharon on every palm-lined beach we could find. Our main go-to was Lydgate Beach with its kid-friendly man-made pools shielded from the open ocean by a ring of boulders. Decked out in our new snorkel gear, the older kids and I dove into this real-life, silent aquarium. We pointed excitedly as chromatic fish flitted around us. Bobbing to the surface for a break, the silence was broken.

A snorkel treasure hunt

"Did you see that huge yellow one?" cried Lucas.

Aaron's head popped up. Yanking the snorkel from his mouth, he exclaimed, "I think I just saw the state fish! How do you say it again?"

Isaac swam over. "You saw a humuhumunukunukuapua'a?! Where?!"

Then they all but disappeared back into the aquarium. I smiled at their discovery of a new world. Gazing beyond the big black boulders at the untamed ocean, I wondered how big of a world it must be.

On one outing, I hollered to the kids, "Dudes, get on over here, Daddy's gonna make sand sculptures outta you!" We cupped our hands together like human backhoes and excavated a wide and deep depression in the beach. While the kids lay on their backs side-by-side in the depression, I bulldozed a thick blanket of sand over their bodies all the way up to their chins.

"Dad, what if there are crabs under here?" objected Eric.

"Hang on, hang on, Mom's gotta snap the picture." I scur-

First "sand burial"

ried away as Sharon clicked the shutter on my masterpiece: five sun-splashed, giggling heads wobbling on the sands of Lydgate Beach (jittery Jordan opted out).

Lydgate had a bonus feature: Kamalani Playground, set in the midst of sprawling grass fields and ironwood pines. "Look over there!" Isaac cried as he pointed at a maze of curious wooden structures across the field. He charged ahead with his siblings close behind.

"Not it," everyone yelled.

"Ha, Lucas is it!"

"Am not!"

"Are too."

Soon a merry game of tag erupted in this mega labyrinth of ramps, stairs, slides, obstacle courses, and castle turrets. Flashes of heads, arms, legs, and bare feet popped up on the upper tiers and reappeared at ground level. I couldn't help myself from adding a little thrill to the chase. I crouched and hid myself in a blind pocket of the maze. As Eric approached, I sprang and growled, "Raar!"

"Ahh," Eric screeched. "Dad, not funny!" Then with a mischievous grin, he said, "Let's get Isaac!"

BASE CAMP HOOLAKO

After a couple of weeks of beach hopping, we intensified our search for long-term lodging. With the gracious help of some newfound friends, the Akitas, we found an affordable month-to-month upstairs duplex on Hoolako Street in Lihue. "We're getting a real house," squealed Katherine, as she rushed in the door. "This is the boys' room," announced Eric. The four older boys dumped out the contents of their duffel bags and organized their new clubhouse. Each quarter had a sleeping bag, blankets, and a pillow followed by a small selection of toys. Katherine and Jordan shared the next room, while Sharon and I took the master bedroom and bath.

We had nothing to put in our living room or kitchen. This was fine with the kids. With a long hallway and nothing to impede velocity, they had an Indy 500 romp room. "Guys, soft feet," I pleaded several times a day. "Poor Theresa." Theresa was our downstairs neighbor—an industrious Korean immigrant who owned two tourist gift shops. She also housed her aged mother, Betty, and a niece, Sujong.

"Theresa, so sorry 'bout the noise." (*Sixteen busy, thumping human feet overhead.*) "We'll try and keep things as calm as possible."

Luckily, she had a soft spot for kids and reassured me, "It's okay."

Because of her soft spot, she hired the kids for odd jobs at home and at her stores. Knocking on the door one day and pointing to Isaac and Eric, she said, "You two good with computers, yeah? I pay you set up new store computer, 'kay?" With the amenities of computer tinkering, spending-money, friendly neighbors, and a romp room to boot, the kids were quite content with our duplex digs.

Despite the joys of minimalism and room to romp, necessities were still necessities. Thus we rounded up a donated couch, a kitchen table, a queen air mattress, and some sleeping pads from more new friends, the Blackburns. More necessities showed up a few weeks later at Nawiliwili Harbor in a large crate we had shipped to ourselves prior to coming. Its arrival under our carport, sitting on the bed of our mini Dodge pickup, turned into an early Christmas.

Using a hammer and flat bar, I pried off the crate lid, and everyone clamored to get a peek inside. Sharon was thrilled to have more kitchenware, and I was glad to get our bikes. Jordan's entire face lit up to see his three-wheeler again. The other kids boomed, "Look, the Legos!" or "Wow, the Ninja Turtles!" As they dug eagerly into the crate, I mulled the paradox, "Happiness is not in getting what you want, but in wanting what you've got." We had accidentally discovered the prime object lesson for teaching this truth. Tuck away the toys in a crate, ship it off on a long round-trip journey and, when it returns, VOILA: instant contentedness with recycled stuff.

CAPTAIN DADDY AND SPAGHETTI

After establishing Base Camp Duplex, we finally settled into a routine. Sharon started her two-week orientation at Wilcox and began to work shifts as they became available. I, on the other hand, took on a role opposite of what I was accustomed to. I became Captain Daddy and spent all day with the kids. This required some personal adaptation. For one thing, I needed to learn how to cook using something besides the microwave. I taught myself how to make spaghetti, proudly boiling noodles and pouring a jar of sauce over them. I even added browned hamburger! Sometimes we ate eggs and toast instead. This seemed to be working until I overheard Isaac murmuring to Eric, "Let me guess, tonight for dinner we are going to have spaghetti."

Eric replied, "Or maybe if we're lucky, eggs and burnt toast."

I grew bolder and branched out into making tacos, a mean stir-fry, and hash browns from hand-grated potatoes (a generous dousing with ketchup did wonders).

My adaptation was deeper though. During the fourteen years of my married life, I had been preoccupied with making a living. It's not that I didn't relish Sharon-and-kid time; in fact, that's what I lived for. However, the demands of providing for a family dictated lots of twelve-hour days in my home improvement business. And so for the three to six months of

Lucas revels in an early island adventure

our getaway, I was going to soak up every possible minute with the kids and Sharon. I did pick up a few little side remodel jobs, managed our rental property on the mainland, and kept a hawk's eye on our budget.

KID COMMENTS

Isaac (13/30)

Shortly after arriving on Kauai, I remember going to the beach all day with no sunscreen, getting torched, and still enjoying it. I remember trying to stay up as late as possible to see what show comes on Nick at Nite after 12:00 a.m. What a feat it would be to make it past 12:00 a.m. I thought.

Our first non-vacation residence on the island had some awesome neighbors. A wonderful Korean lady named Theresa and her mother lived below. One day Theresa's sweet octogenarian mother braved the stairs up to our apartment and invited us kids down for lunch. This was the first time I remember being exposed to the pungent aroma of *kimchi* (pickled cabbage). We didn't know quite how to eat it and since she only spoke Korean, that made consumption pretty difficult. Over the years I have gotten used to kimchi's sharp flavor and now actually enjoy it. I owe it all to this kind impromptu lunch invite.

Katherine (4/21)

There are two things I remember from the Hoolako house: putting on my favorite dress to play in the rain (it was quite the occasion—warm rain!) and trying *li hing mui* for the first time. My local friend who lived next door offered it to me. Looked like candy—good, right? But it was candy covered in salty, dried plum powder. I looked like a baby trying real food for the first time. I spit it out. I thought my friend was crazy!

But now when I'm at school on the mainland, whenever mom asks what I want in packages from home, my first answer is always *"li hing mui* mango!!" Now I'm the crazy island girl!

CHAPTER THREE

Kauai Study Abroad: The Land

I am standing speechless at Kauai's Kalalau Lookout. An emerald fluted pali (volcanic cliff) is merging itself into an azure ocean and sky. Ribbon-like waterfalls weep from the pali's side. The stroke of reverence I feel for this scene has matched that of my all-time favorite, the Sawtooth Peaks of Idaho towering above the headwaters of the Salmon River. The kids are chasing back and forth along the railing and seem actually interested in the view.

"Look!" Eric calls out. He has spotted our first full Hawaiian rainbow, arching over the Pacific horizon—a metaphor of the promising season in the sun that lies ahead.

Of course there was the important question of what to do about the kids' education during our getaway. Sharon answered this when she mustered her mommy powers and academic talent and created "Study Abroad Kauai." The kids would study Hawaii firsthand and maintain core-subject progress using textbooks from the Salvation Army. On the days Sharon worked, I administered her assignments. I also instituted a rigorous exercise program to whip the kids into shape. "Okay everybody, let's begin with 25 pushups and 25 sit ups!" I barked to some brisk music.

Kalalau Overlook

"Awww, Mom never made us do these!" came the morning barrage.

"Just do 'em, and you'll thank me for it later," I fired back.

Meanwhile, Study Abroad Kauai launched into full swing, and we set out to experience the island's history, geography, and culture face-to-face. "Okay everyone, today's a road trip day. We're off to see Kauai," I announced. "So what'll it be, north or south?"

"Does it matter?" wisecracked Lucas, "It's an island, so let's make a loop."

"Nice thought, son, though I think you know better. In fact, here's our first geography review of the day. Remember the Na Pali Coast on the west side? It's a fortress of cliffs, so no road there."

"Dad, let's go north and hit that end of the road beach," offered Isaac.

"Yeah, that place is awesome!" appealed a hopeful Eric.

"Okay, we'll do some swimming, but remember our focus is to learn stuff," I reminded. We piled in the van, northbound for the end of the road—Ke'e Beach.

Enroute, Sharon, the teacher, reviewed some Kauai basics. "Listen up, 'cause I'm gonna test you guys on this later." Attention secured, she speed read and expounded, "Kauai is 582 square miles and is geologically the oldest of the main Hawaiian islands. 300 miles to the southeast and positioned on the same drifting tectonic plate is the youngest, still-forming Big Island. It now sits on the same lava hot spot on the ocean floor which anciently formed Kauai." As we passed beneath the traffic lights of busy Kapaa, she continued, "Oh, and get this, Kauai is known as The Unconquered Island. It was never militarily conquered by King Kamehameha. Oh . . . and here's a little drama for you. Most of his invasion canoes sunk in 1796 in a storm while crossing the Kauai channel."

"Well, there's some cool action," a backseater perked up.

Entering the outskirts of Hanalei thirty minutes later, Sharon and I gawked at the backdrop of soaring mist-crowned *palis* draped at the valley's edge. Dangling from the *palis'* sides were white satiny threads of waterfalls. A river coursing through the valley's emerald taro fields collected these threads and wove them into teal-colored Hanalei bay.

Hoping to stoke kid curiosity, we bantered, "Have you ever seen anything as green as these taro fields?"

"I know, I know, check out the kayakers on the river."

Sadly, in the backseat was only chit chat about shave ice shacks and who was squashing who. "Okay, everyone out. I want a picture of us by these taro fields," ordered the teacher. The kids had learned never to argue with her about picture taking, so as the camera clicked, their eye rolling turned into dutiful happy faces.

Leaving Hanalei we entered a go-cart course of serpentine curves and one-lane bridges leading to Haena. As driver, I had to muster deep willpower. Keeping my eyes fixed on the narrow lanes instead of on the beach vistas peeking through the ironwood pines wasn't easy. Crossing the single lane bridges also required attention. Posted signs laid down protocol: "Local courtesy 5-7 cars."

After a bit of beach romping and snorkeling, we headed back to Hanalei and the nearest shave ice shack to reward good behavior. Ascending to Princeville and passing Kilauea, we entered a lush coastal plain framed by eternal Pacific blue on one side, and the serrated ridges of Mt. Waialeale on the other. One backseater, anxious to re-enter civilization, urged, "Dad, the speed limit says 50. Step on it!"

I teased back, "I'm givin' it all she's got, Captain!" Soon enough, backseaters were dropping not-so-subtle hints about stopping for snacks at the WalMart or McDonald's we were passing. We were now back in civilization.

A road trip to Kauai's west side had its own unique flavor. "Gang, Mom and I want to take you on a field trip to see The Grand Canyon of the Pacific today."

"Aw, Dad, we've been there like three times already."

"Now, now, remember, you don't know what you don't

Sunset at "End of the Road" Beach

know. And we can have a picnic and play kickball at the Kokee Meadow. So get ready."

Daypacks bulging with diversions and snacks, we exited Lihue on Kaumualii Highway. Vast fields of sugarcane flanked us on either side of the road. After passing Knudsen Gap, I made a surprise detour left into the fairytale tunnel of eucalyptus trees leading to Koloa. A backseater fretted, "Faster, Dad, there's s'posed to be a scary ghost lady that lives in here, and if you have any pork in the car, she'll get you!" (Hawaii is full of legends about *menehunes* and night marchers—forest dwarves and ghosts of departed warriors.)

I winked at Sharon, "Honey, what kind of lunch meat did you pack in our picnic?"

"Uh-oh, I think it was ham," she winked back.

Retreating safely out of the tunnel, and back onto the highway, we passed Kalaheo. The landscape was now coffee fields. The teacher filled us in, "Did you know that Kauai has over four million coffee trees and is the largest coffee producer in the state?"

Pointing oceanward, I offered my two cents, "Yeah, and that over there is Port Allen. The smoke stacks belong to the big diesel generators that make Kauai's electricity." Now coming into view were Hanapepe Town and arid accents of cacti growing on red dirt hillsides.

Sharon asked, "What's Hanapepe known for?"

"Art capital of Kauai," proudly answered Lucas. "And it has that rad swinging bridge!"

"Can we pleeease go on it again?" sung a chorus of backseaters. I glanced at Sharon. With the teacher's nod, we parked the van and scampered onto the rickety reeling structure. Everyone was digging this except Jordan whose face turned pale midpoint of the bridge, spooked by the specter of the muddy river below. His whimpering produced a concurrent rescue from sympathetic Sharon and an uptick in rocking of the bridge from goading siblings.

On the outskirts of Waimea, the teacher directed. "Okay, I know we've been there, done that, but for history sake let's review Russian Fort."

"Noooo," came a backseat vocal barrage, as I pulled into the state historical site.

"Whoopee. It's a big pile of boring boul-

Swinging bridge in Hanapepe

ders," complained Eric. I secretly agreed.

"Do you remember why and when it was built?" Sharon quizzed. Silence.

"Okay, then, let's get out and read the plaques again." Once the plaques about the Russian explorers who came in the early 1800's were dutifully read, the kids and I then guided the teacher back into the van. We made a quick escape to the highway.

Now in view of Waimea's hillsides, I offered a geography insight of my own, "If I didn't know we were in Hawaii, I'd think we were back in Idaho." The dry grass clinging to the black hillsides mimicked scenes of the Snake River lava plain where I had grown up.

In Waimea Town, we ignored the tempting invite of seventeen-mile-long Polihale Beach farther to the west and

Waipoo Falls and the "Grand Canyon of the Pacific"

branched north onto a steep switchback mountain road. After much tummy sloshing, a backseat voice begged, "Daddy, can we please stop? This road is making me sick!"

Pulling over, I announced, "Very well then, let's go have a looksee." Walking to the railing of an overlook, we entered Waimea Canyon's living art show where towering walls of weather-beaten rocks pigmented in red, yellow, and brown coalesced on a dream-like canvas. Brushed onto the canvas were a pastel blue sky and swatches of green cutting the borders of plunging Waipoo Falls.

"Yup, it's just like they say—Grand Canyon of the Pacific," Aaron spouted off the nickname. I detected a hint of parroting in what may have been his fourth such statement.

KID COMMENTS

Katherine (4/21)

Outings were a grand but stressful thing for me. I changed my clothes multiple times before I found the right outfit for a road trip to the North shore or the Waimea Canyon. My brothers never seemed to have that problem! Being able to just don surf shorts every day of their lives must've been nice. After the right outfit was put together, then began the packing for the long trip ahead. I must have forgotten how long real road trips were because I packed like I was headed to Africa. A pillow, snacks, and a Boxcar Children book were necessities.

Jordan (2/19)

Though for much of my life I was usually more than happy to hike and camp, I vividly remember, oddly, hating the drive-to, park-and-walk-twenty-steps type overlooks. Yes, they were gorgeous, but after the first five or less seconds, I grouchily asked myself, "We've been there, done that so many times already, why are we here again?" That's when I'd more often than not resort to chasing the nearby chickens or just flat out pout (usually the latter). If ever the question got posed whether we wanted to stop at one of the gorgeous overlooks, I would make sure my opinion was known. Despite my adamant protests, we somehow ended up stopping at the overlooks and gawking at the some of the prettiest scenery in the world. Life for a Kauai island dweller is just hard sometimes.

CHAPTER FOUR

Kauai Study Abroad: The People and Culture

We are cruising down the road when a monument with an engraved slogan catches my eye. "Sharon, did you notice that monument, something about Kauai, many peoples?"

"Yeah, I've seen it several places on the island. Actually it says, 'One island, many peoples, all Kauaiians.'"

What a fitting slogan for the fascinating collage of neighborly people we have mingled with during our sojourn, I muse. The field of surnames is eclectic and vast: Nakaahiki, Raralio, Ching, Kakazu, Thronas, and Ward to name a few. I smile to think that at least for now our surname has blended into this collage.

Lining Kauai's roadsides are her 60,000-plus local residents, her very soul. Mainlanders have asked me if it's hard for a *malahine* (outsider) to find acceptance in the local culture. Speaking for me alone, I would have to say yes and no. Some native Hawaiians have shared with me frustrations about their long history of unfairness from immigrants to their islands. Others have taken into account the balancing fair shakes and opportunities that the outside world has brought to them. Setting human folly and political factors aside, most seem grateful to be part of a free and protected land that provides one of the highest standards of living among remote Pacific island chains. And while it is sometimes hard for a caucasian *malahine* to earn a local's trust, there are some proven secrets to acceptance.

My good friend, Steve, who adopted Kauai as his home, once coached us when we entered a neighborhood party, "Listen, just eat the food, even if you don't like it, and laugh at the jokes, funny or not." It proved to be spot on advice for getting adopted—at least topically—into Kauai's family. And what a fascinating family they are—a patchwork quilt of Hawaiian, Pacific Island, Asian, and European cultures—sewn together through plantation economics, missionary work, and tropical migrations.

Most are mindful of their melting pot heritage and will proudly reel off their genealogy if you ask them. At first I didn't believe locals who assured me it's not impolite to ask, but one day I mustered the nerve, "Nani, what's your family tree like?"

"I'm half Filipino, a quarter *Podagee* (Portuguese) an eighth Hawaiian, and an eighth Chinese," she rattled off with a smile.

Oddly, it's also not awkward or impolite in some households to crack jokes about one's own ethnicity. It seems to be a celebration of diversity to poke a little fun at one's own cultural quirks.

DAKINE PIDGIN

As a part of our study abroad we learned a foreign language (sort of). A few visiting friends who had never visited Hawaii asked me if we were learning to speak Hawaiian. "Sure," I said. "Do you want to hear some?" I rattled off, "Hanalei kilauea kapaa lihue kalaheo hanapepe waimea kekaha." Our friends were impressed, but then I noticed Sharon giving me the eye to fess up. "Naw, only kidding, I was reeling off a bunch of Kauai towns from the map in my head."

Some locals do speak Hawaiian and there is a growing resurgence of learning it. However, most speak a relaxed mix of English and Hawaiian Pidgin—a dialect that borrows words and phrases from Hawaii's amalgam of languages and cultures. Here are a few of the most useful words and phrases.

For directions, *mauka* refers to the mountain side of the road; *makai*, the ocean side. *On-island* or *off-island* refers to one's travel status. *Pau* means done; *pau hana* means done with work. *Aloha Friday* means done with work for the week-end (usually spoken with great enthusiasm). *Choke* means a lot of something; *puka* means hole; *slippahs* means flip-flops; and *bumbye* means be patient, it'll happen later (much later if a mechanic is speaking). *Keiki* means child. *Kane* means gentle-men, and *wahine* means woman—very useful to know when restrooms are identified only in Hawaiian. *Mine's one,* or *her's one* indicates possession. *Grinds* means food, and *grinds* that are *ono* (delicious) disappear rather quickly at luaus. The word *dakine* is a marvelous linguistic fix-all. Brain-cramp? Forget a term or a name? No problem! Substitute *dakine.* It'll mean whatever you want it to mean!

Grammar in Pidgin is as laid back as napping on the beach. Forget about English's tricky tenses, articles, and prep-ositions (the kids loved this). "*We go Vegas*" cuts to the chase and means "We're going to Las Vegas" (the "ninth island" where many Hawaiians seem to go for their getaways). Where a plural should be added, it is left off, and where it shouldn't be added, strangely, it is sometimes: "*K, gentlemens, time fo' go work.*"

Even if a *malahine* can pick up Pidgin, he would still be detected as a non-local speaker. It is near impossible to imitate the distinct accent locals are immersed in from birth. It's still fun, however, to amuse/annoy local friends by buzzing them with some Pidgin. "Hey, Benny try translate this," I challenged my friend, "*Puka pau choke ono kine grinds dakine brah.*" (Translation: "Hole done a lot of delicious food whatever brother.") Wearing a half-stumped grin, he sputtered, "Wait a minute, what did you just say?" before realizing I had fed him a blurb of Pidgin nonsense.

A FILIPINO FEAST AND FIREWORKS

Peering further into the cultural kaleidoscope, we discovered New Year's in Hawaii. From our upstairs apartment we had a clear view of the Mendoza home across the street. They were our Filipino landlords, and they loved to celebrate the coming in of the new year. We were invited to their family's 1998 New Year's Eve party in their carport. From the safe perch of our balcony we observed a massive crowd of revelers assembling and were timid to go. But curiosity nibbled away until we moseyed downstairs, crossed the street, and entered the fray.

Above the festive roar, Lina, the matriarch, introduced us, "Everybody, these are our guests, the Stennetts." She then invited us to dive into the massive potluck of Hawaiian/Filipino food and desserts that covered table after table. Glutting ourselves on these (a welcome reprieve from Daddy's spaghetti), we engaged the Mendoza clan in talking story. Lina's son, Rudy, grabbed my ear. He was a retired USAF major, and had lived worldwide. There was much to discuss. All around us, everyone was laughing and forgetting life's cares for awhile. Even the kids were smiling and talking with *aunties* and *uncles* (what you call your elders in Hawaii) in between bites of *ono grinds*.

Right before midnight, Lina's son, Marco, went to the

middle of the street and set up a tall step ladder from which he suspended a string of ten thousand firecrackers. Then he set them ablaze. We cupped our hands to our ears to deaden the ear-splitting staccato. Through the strobe light flickers, our kids resembled bouncing caricatures of laughing *menehunes*. As the fuse hissed to its end, it bit into a ferocious wad of gunpowder, igniting a finale thunderclap and flash. Up and down the street the neighbors mirrored the mayhem. As the phosphoric phenomenon faded, we found ourselves happily alive and grinning at each other through a thick fog of smoke. Happy New Year everyone—Hawaii style!

This new culture of food, friendliness, and firecrackers, wrapped in a blanket of tropical warmth, was enchanting. I couldn't help comparing it to the previous New Year's Eve in Bear Lake. I had stepped outside to get some air around the stroke of midnight. Greeting me was a curtain of dead silence and freezing cold. Suddenly the crack of a hunting rifle pierced the silence. A merrymaker had fired off a single, celebratory round into the air. And then it was simply quiet again. "Huh, so that's it," I muttered to myself.

THE CHINGS

Friendship with the Mendoza clan led to friendship with an empty-nester couple, Lester and Tomiko Ching. They welcomed us to the island by inviting us to dinner at their house in the untamed Huleia River Valley. Eager to talk story with them, we drove into the countryside near Lihue, descending gradually into the thick jungle surrounding their home.

Hearing our car arrive in the driveway, Lester emerged from a tall patch of buffalo grass carrying a machete and wearing knee-high irrigation boots. Tomiko appeared on the deck by the front door of the house and politely waved to us. They were a fascinatingly odd match: a petite Japanese woman who always kept her surroundings in strict realms of refinement, juxtaposed with a come-as-you-are Hawaiian farm boy. They were married while he was serving in the military in post-World War II Japan.

While Tomiko was putting final touches of elegance on dinner, Lester led us on a guided tour across his ten-acre property. His guru oration on the native and nonnative flora, punctuated by machete gestures, held our attention. "Those are haole koa trees. Great feed for cattle and goats, but grows like crazy. It'll take over everything if you let it." We strolled past a titan monkeypod tree, fallen yet still clinging to life through its partially intact root system. "This poor fella met his doom, along with my house, when Hurricane Iniki danced over Kauai in '92. There's no winning against a Category Four."

HULA A LA JUNGLE

When we arrived at the river, Lester pointed to a deep spot. "There's where I was baptized as a boy." He proceeded to machete off oblong, arm-length ti plant leaves and a short length of vine. Stitching the ti leaves onto the vine, a jungle-spun hula skirt appeared. "Anyone for hula?" Lester invited. Giggling Eric bounded forward and tied the vine sash around his waist. Lester began to softly sing, "Lovely hula hands, graceful as the birds in motion, gliding like the gulls over the ocean." Eric mimicked amateur moves in rhythm and was soon joined by his siblings. I glanced over at Sharon, ensconced in this timeless Hawaiian setting. Her pretty smile conveyed the message, "Andy, how lucky could we possibly be?"

Meandering on, we entered a pocket of jungle where sturdy vines hung from tall trees. Lester threw out a tempting hint, "Do you kids like Tarzan?" Without hesitation, Isaac, Eric, Lucas, and Aaron ran full throttle and launched themselves onto vines—only to discover that Tarzan treetop travel was a myth. Aaron felt especially "let down" when his vine snapped, leaving him with a sore keister.

Later, back at the house, Lester fetched his bamboo fruit picking pole and began plucking oranges from a tree on the patio's edge. Lowering the pole, he prompted Jordan, "Get your orange out." Jordan excitedly complied and put orange after orange into a bag, not realizing this was actually work. When the bag was full, Lester handed it to me to take home. Accepting his gift, I said, "Wow, kids, look at these beautiful oranges. Lester, thank you!" We were becoming acclimated to Hawaii's frequent manifestations of old-time generosity—and learning to accept them without embarrassment.

Kauai Study Abroad learns from Lester Ching

Tomiko then ushered us inside and sat us down to a spread of five-star cuisine in the jungle. "Everyone, enjoy," was her simple and polite invitation. After our feast, Lester, aka Mr. Golf, brought out an indoor putting cup and patiently taught putting basics to the kids. As we prepared to leave, Tomiko presented a gift to Sharon—a kimono from Japan, and demonstrated the precise ceremonial method of folding it.

Oddly, in the midst of this beautiful politeness, I felt the urge to ask someone, "Say there, can you please pinch me real hard? I gotta know if the Chings, and the Tarzan vines, and the kimono, and the lovely hula hands, and the . . . everything else we've experienced in Kauai is not a big snow-trench hallucination. And even if it is, I think I'll just stay in it forever."

NIGHTLIFE ON KAUAI

Mingling with the Chings and other locals, we discovered a divide of opinion concerning prioritizing one's time for different cultural activities. For some, it's all about the hula at the luau. For others it's all about the *grinds* at the luau. For others yet, it's not about the hula or the *grinds* at all. What it's really all about is fishing. Many Kauaians diligently and patiently fish from the shore with hooks and with nets. Others choose boating and trolling the open seas for their catch. But the hard-core fisherman do it face-to-face, underneath the water, at night, with a spear.

Not long after we had arrived on Kauai, one fisherman, Dale Akita (a caring school teacher, husband, and father by day), announced to me, "Steve Alvarez and I are doing a night dive on Friday. Wanna come?"

I was intrigued about the diving part, but weirded out about the night part. At the risk of seeming naive (and chicken), I asked, "So, is it really necessary to go at night?"

Sensing my uneasiness, he replied, "That's when the fish are sleepy and become easier targets."

Game for a cultural dare, I signed on. Around 8:00 p.m. they picked me up, and we drove forty minutes to Moloaa Beach. Steve rummaged around in the bed of his pickup and handed me a wadded up wetsuit, fins, and mask. "Here ya go. Try these on for size." Dale gave me a hefty dive light powered by eight D cell batteries and a wicked four-pronged spear, called a Hawaiian sling.

Reading my novice body language, Dale gave me the idiot's course in cocking and firing my sling (probably in part to protect his own hide). "Here, loop the elastic around your bicep, pull the spear back along your forearm, and grip it firmly in your hand. When you see a big fish and can close the distance, let it rip." He tacked on, "Stay on our heels and inside the reef, and you'll be fine."

Amidst pale moonlight, I followed my friends down across the safe, sandy beach, donned my fins and mask, and backed slowly into the dark, cold water. This was definitely a time for cowboying up Hawaii-style. As I plied through the water, I began to wonder if they had pranked me by giving me a mask with a built-in fogger. Also, I wanted to ask my friends a question now racing through my mind: had they never heard about all the sharks living in the ocean? Not wanting to appear unmanly, I trusted their instincts. They must know—surely they must know—and surely they had a viable anti-shark plan.

The water was rough that night, and our bodies pitched up and down with the surging of the tide. In spots it was eerily murky. I quickly jettisoned my grandiose goal of spearing a big fish for tomorrow's dinner and worked on more attainable goals: keeping water out of my lungs and not losing sight of Dale and Steve. They were like a pair of water mutants, half human and half fish, intrepidly weaving into the notches of the reef, skillfully firing their spears and bagging prey.

Despite my uneasiness in these surreal watery corridors, I found some relaxation in beholding the many odd creatures passing through the beam of my light. Suddenly, I spotted a slithering snake-like eel, which ruined the mood. This gave me an unsettling epiphany. Since I was in their domain sizing them up as a potential meal, might not these innocent looking fishies also be sizing me up as a potential meal? That's when my Hawaiian spear became, in my mind, not a tool of capture, but a weapon to defend myself.

Further unsettling was seeing Steve get high-centered. A heave of water receded suddenly, leaving him sprawled belly down on the reef. Though unnerving at first, beholding a large man wearing a snorkel mask while wielding a spear—and flailing helplessly on a reef in the middle of the night—did supply some comic relief.

About an hour later, Steve, Dale, and I were safely back on shore. Land never felt so good! On the ride home I sleepily processed the night's events. The meaning of the old saying, "like a fish out of water," was clearer now than ever. Having assumed that role in reverse, "like a human in water," I could truly empathize with all the poor little fish ever caught in such a dilemma.

Arriving back in Lihue, I thanked my new pals for their hospitality. I thought I saw them give each other a sly grin. "Andy, you were a good sport. You know, it gets easier each time you go," Steve said.

Exiting the pickup, I nodded and said, "Yup, see you guys next time," knowing full well that this was my first—and *last*—night dive.

Kauai and her charming people were endearing themselves to us. With each passing day, Bear Lake began to seem like a distant planet. The kids had made some friends, and no one minded trading in long pants for surf shorts. Even I opted to shelve my Wranglers and hiking lace-ups in lieu of shorts and flip-flops. In the midst of these easy-going ways, we began to feel comfortable with staying at least the full six months of our season in the sun.

KID COMMENTS

Isaac (13/30)

New Years was crazy. People blew everything up. Great food. Hawaiians really know how to celebrate. My favorite Pidgin phrase of all time is "broke da mout." This phrase is used when eating something delicious. "Ho brah, these grinds [food] broke da mout." I'm not sure where this came from—"the food is so good it broke my mouth" doesn't seem like it would indicate deliciousness, but in Pidgin this is par for the course. When I brought my girlfriend to Hawaii for the first time, my mom told her we were going to get dinner and *pupus*. *Pupus* is Pidgin for oeur d'oeuvres, but of course it phonetically sounds like "poo poo." Needless to say, my girlfriend was relieved when she found out it was not the latter definition.

Aaron (7/24)

My first New Year's celebration was a bit of an education. I remember grabbing a serving of what I thought was fried chicken ... only as I bit into it, it was much more rubbery. A closer look revealed I was gnawing on tentacles. After asking a question or two, I confirmed my suspicion that I was eating octopus for the first time in my life.

Katherine (4/21)

Pidgin was a life-saver at times. Forget a word? Use dakine. Forget a name? Just say aunty or uncle. One time I was at the beach and I desperately needed to ask my friend's mom something, but I couldn't remember her name! That's when I recalled the whole aunty/uncle thing. "Hey aunty?" "Yes?" Success! As I got older, though, it took on a much deeper meaning. I came to love that I could call anyone older than me aunty or uncle. It meant that they were my family. Also, I'll never forget the first time a kid called me aunty. It freaked me out.

CHAPTER FIVE

The Jungle House

"Whaaat?" Isaac asks loudly.

"Can you please turn it up?" Sharon repeats. We are trying to watch a movie, but the TV's volume is getting trumped by the thundering rain falling on the house's uninsulated metal roof.

"It's already at max volume!" shouts Isaac.

I intercede as best I can, "How 'bout we pause the movie till the rain calms down." It's another spoiler, one of many that seems to go with living in a quirky jungle house.

No sooner had the lemon-yellow sun risen on my family daydream than it was due to set. Our six-month boundary had arrived, and we were at a crossroads. Should we linger on a bit longer or go back to our normal life on the mainland? The deep snow on our farm would be melted by now and the glorious alpine spring of Bear Lake would be in full swing. That meant I could go to work building Sharon's log home and make a fresh start at recovering from gypsyness. Also, going back made the most financial sense.

Just when we were ready to buy one-way tickets home, a fortuitous coconut dropped out of the Hawaiian sky—an opportunity that tipped the balance in favor of staying. A local attorney friend, Roger, mentioned to me that he was scouting for a live-in property manager for a vacant house tucked away in a two-acre pocket of jungle. "It's in Lihue, a short walk from

Kalapaki Beach," he related. "There's even a pasture next door stocked with grazing cows and horses. I think Idaho-boy you will like it."

"Sounds amazing. Is there a catch?"

"Only catch is that it's an *ohana* property. It's been willed down to so many descendants that there is no clear title of ownership. My office is working on the legal wrinkles, and eventually it'll be sold."

"Any estimate on when that'll be?"

"Six months would be the soonest. In the meantime you and your family can live there for a small monthly rent as long as you maintain the house, agree to tear down some of the old shacks, and keep the grounds up."

This seemed both doable and enticing. I hurried home to share the news of this freshly-fallen coconut with Sharon.

We factored the news of the *ohana* house into our ongoing debate about extending our getaway. The pros and cons we had scribbled out on a spiral notebook always concluded with a single question: what would it hurt to stay a little longer? After all, we could financially swing it with this new frugal living arrangement, cash flow from Sharon's nursing, rental income from our mainland home, and my little remodeling jobs. Bear Lake was still there, and the log house could wait.

The final incentive to linger on came as I was having a heart-to-heart chat with Isaac about our pending decision. I wasn't really expecting him to voice an opinion, so I was surprised to see him smile and say, "We should stay, Dad."

That struck a heart string with me because, above all else, I have always simply wanted my family to be happy. I told Sharon about my chat with Isaac, and reasoned, "Dear, the kids are just plain happy to be here!"

"I completely agree," she said. "What else can we do but hang loose a bit longer and see where things will go?" Thus,

Sharon and I shook hands with our attorney friend and planned to move our brood into the *ohana* house. Leaving Roger's office, Sharon said, "I wanna go see it first. I wanna know what we're getting into."

"Buckle in," I said. "Sounds like it might be a wild ride!"

From the moment we made the steep hairpin turn off of the highway to check out our new habitat, I sensed an agreeable shift in tenor. In the rearview mirror was bustling Lihue, and appearing through the windshield was old-Hawaii: a tunnel of trees and a 160-yard pockmarked lane leading to some simple wooden houses topped with rusting metal roofs. One of those houses was to be ours.

Parking in front of the house Roger had described, I glanced nervously at Sharon. "Dear, looks like this is it." I turned the ignition off and pulled the pickup's door handle.

The hairpin turn to the lane

The release brought a flood of quiet. Even the distant crow of roosters seemed to drown in it. The carport gravel grumbled under our feet as we made our way to the rickety screen door.

Upon entering the house, my inviolable carpenter's sense of plumb, level, and square was immediately assaulted. Although made mostly of modern materials, the house had been hastily ad libbed atop the splintered ruins of its pre-Hurricane Iniki ancestor. The thought of daily walking on systemic sloping floors bordered by slanting walls made me wince. But the improviser and economiser within me spoke of compromise. As long as things were kept tidy, safe, and functional, I could turn a blind eye to the aggravating swoops and slopes.

I continued my survey as Sharon continued hers. I was relieved that the basics were there: culinary water, showers, flushing toilets, and electricity. "Nooo!" I scoffed as I traced the water supply from the county meter to a wimpy PVC pipe hung loosely on the house's exterior with nails and wire. The pipe meandered its way into two small side-by-side bathrooms, then into the kitchen, and finally into the water heater on the open back porch. Wastewater drained into an antiquated cesspool, a deep and wide cylindrical pit covered by a heavy disc of cement. Gray water from the washing machine was diverted into a patch of grass out in the jungle.

Under a jumble of mismatched, conjoining roofs was a 20' x 20' living room, three bedrooms, two bathrooms, a kitchen, and a dubbed-on screened-in porch. The country boy in me concluded that the decor wasn't horrible. The dazed look on poor Sharon's face said otherwise as we met in the tilting hall. "Seriously?!" she disclosed her ambivalence, as she gestured at the old carpet and yellowing walls.

Leading me to the kitchen, she pointed at the termite-riddled sink pedestal and three feet of counter space. "The rusted range matches the decor so perfectly," she quipped. She had been down this dusty trail with me before, living in fixer-upper investment houses.

I gave my best pep talk, "Dear, it's only for a short season, till we figure out the next step. It's cheap, and the beach is practically in our backyard." Apparently, my last sentence became the dealmaker.

She gave a wry smile. "Backyard beach, huh?"

"Yeah," I hopefully smiled back.

"Well, what's that real estate phrase you're always saying?" she set me up. "It's location, location, location. And if we are located here, I plan to be located at the beach—a lot!"

The ohana house

"Deal!"

With Sharon firmly on board, we mobilized our munchkins for a quick makeover before moving in.

"We have to do what?!" whined Lucas and Aaron.

"Yup, sweep and vacuum out this entire house and the porches—especially get rid of any dead bugs so Mom doesn't see 'em."

"I can't wash all these walls by myself," protested Eric.

"You don't have to. Isaac will help. And after that we get to have even more fun—we get to paint. And after that we get to steam clean the carpets. It's a such a rad machine; you're gonna love it."

While Sharon managed the cleaning, I set to work in the kitchen extending the counter space, fixing the plumbing, and building shelves. After rolling a fresh coat of gleaming white paint over every wall, we added the final touch—mismatched styles of second-hand and even home-made furniture. We were now ready to move in.

Fitting six kids in two small bedrooms required some creativity and diplomacy. We gave Katherine the bedroom next to our room and fitted it with a queen bed from the hotel furniture outlet. Migrant Jordan sometimes slept on a mini-bed in Katherine's room, but usually camped on a couch or wherever his energy ballon finally deflated. Isaac, Eric, Lucas, and Aaron got stacked into bunk beds in the 12' x 12' bedroom next to the carport. It was a snug fit, yet the evolving mishmash of posters plastered on the walls and ceiling of their little man cave signaled they were making it work. And amidst the caveman clutter of Legos and laundry, a pact of lasting camaraderie was born. Meanwhile, poor Katherine had to endure a jealous barb here and there. "All bow! Here comes Queen Kates with her OWN queen bed and a room as big as China."

A 3D NATURE DOCUMENTARY

Most of the house's windows were jalousies, but in some of the window frames there were merely screens—enhancing the hang-loose mood throughout. In the living room was a large picture window that became a personal contemplation and family bonding site. It framed a living Van Gogh of velvety green leaves interwoven with subtle hues of gray bark, flecked with clean white plumeria blossoms. At times our Van Gogh window was stroked with crystal hues of rain or accented with the red combs of roosting wild roosters. Peering deeper into the collage, we detected a spacious, grassy area often dotted with playing children.

The picture window also became an unexpected source of cinematic bonding. The wall space beneath it happened to be the best spot for the TV. One evening movie was interrupted when Isaac exclaimed, "Hey look at the geckos on the window! It's a live nature documentary!" Indeed it was. From our comfy couches, we could either watch the sappy chick flick the girls had picked or we could watch "The Gecko Kill Zone" in vivid 3D. Lured in by the emanating light, flying insects landed on the window, signaling the tiny ninja-like lizards to fade into kill-box formation. The gecko in the blind-spot locus then swooped in and snapped up the unlucky bug in his tightly clenched jaws.

This flurry elicited a wide range of viewer responses. Naturally, we felt a stab of pity for the prey, but, almost morbidly,

Gecko "kill zone"

we applauded the A-team geckos as pest-control allies. There was also comic relief when a gecko snagged a jumbo moth. After enduring a jarring minute of the mad flailing wings of an undying prey, alas, the gecko was forced to surrender its coveted feast.

THE MOAT

There were but two major issues with the house: flooding and leaking. Behind the house was a hill covered in thick jungle. Whenever it rained, and I mean RAINED, runoff channeled itself into streams and rushed down the hill. I always worried about this causing a problem, and on New Year's Day 2005, my worries were confirmed. After a night of cloudbursts, we greeted the new year with muddy puddles of water in the house. Standing on soaked carpet, Sharon gloomily muttered, "Happy New Year, Hubby." After a party-pooper cleanup, the kids and I dug a safety moat along the back of the house that prevented future floods.

The other major problem with the house concerned its maddening metal roof. Many were the torments inflicted on us by this hovering bully. For starters, there was the annoyance of living inside an echo chamber. Each noise on the roof above was amplified to maximum volume down below (most houses in Hawaii do not have ceiling insulation). The plop of a dainty Java plum berry from overhanging branches registered as the thud of a baseball, and nighttime feral cat fights as the brawling of tigers (jungle cats fancied the roof for their cage matches). Wild chickens scratching and pecking in the early morning sounded like a discordant troupe of tap dancers. And, of course, there was the sound of the pounding rain.

The major inconvenience, though, was battling leaks in the roof. Most of these leaks could be traced to the acidic

Eric sweeping the roof

effects of Java plum berries. At first I ignored the berries, humming to myself, "Don't worry, be happy; it's a jungle house." Bad plan! The metal eventually rusted through in many places. It became like a game of whack-a-mole, patch one leak, and another would pop up elsewhere. I learned that even the tiniest roof hole in a downpour lets in a strangely disproportionate volume of water.

Eventually, the answer to our problem came down to full replacement of the rusted-out metal sheets. And as preventative maintenance, I chainsawed back the Java plum branches and assigned the older children to routinely sweep all debris off the roof. After getting pounded by our roofing bully for so long, the wise words of my fourth-grade teacher, Mrs. Rowlins, came back to haunt me, "Children, never put off until tomorrow what you can do today."

In time, the jungle house grew into a cozy home as the sounds of rainstorms, Java plum plops, and cat scuffles blended in with the everyday clacking of dishes, the clatter of legos, and the laughter of kids. It became our own music hall where the notes of this curious jungle symphony filled the air.

Many relatives and friends visited and even stayed with us in our music hall over the years. At first, this was worrisome, especially for Sharon. The simplicity of the house prompted her to temper visitor expectations with a standard disclaimer, "Just so you know, we're but one step above camping." Surprisingly, most of our visitors seemed to enjoy the quirky ambience. One visiting brother-in-law, gazing out our Van Gogh window, raved, "This is fascinating! I can't believe this view is right outside your window." I agreed.

KID COMMENTS

Isaac (13/30)

The weirdest thing I ever did to keep our house afloat was when Dad told us to go and "jack up the house." I was young and had only heard this in a car context, so I was surprised it could be applied to houses as well. He gave Eric and me a bottle jack and some wood blocks and then showed us a place in the hallway that was lower than the rest of the house. And by lower, I don't mean nouveau-architecture-design-done-on-purpose-to-be-edgy lower, I mean, scary-something-structurally-important-is-no-longer-present lower. Anyway, we dutifully crawled under the house, positioned the blocks and jack, and literally jacked up the house. Walking through the hallway was much more pleasant after this.

Eric (11/28)

The Jungle Patch house was definitely sketch. I remember helping my dad clean it out, and I thought it was just a project of his. Turned out we moved into it, and well, I guess I kinda grew up there! We made it work; it was a tight fit in the boys' room, but I am so happy we were so close. I feel like my brothers are my best friends. I remember being always a bit sketch about having only screens as windows in our room.

Aaron (7/24)

We had been in a few houses before we found the Jungle Patch, but this house was by far the best. The small jungle house was surrounded by all sorts of trees and plants. This was heaven for my siblings and me because we now had all of this for our playground. The home itself wasn't anything spectacular in terms of size or looks, but it was home, and I loved it.

CHAPTER SIX

The Jungle Patch

Sharon and I are pondering the tangled walls of jungle surrounding our new home. I sense she is having an aha moment. "Hah, I always found it hard to believe that a huge place like Angkor Wat in Cambodia could somehow up and get swallowed by the jungle. Now I totally get it! The Jungle Patch . . . that's what we'll call this place." She has always had a gift for choosing nicknames that perfectly snapshot her loved ones and her surroundings. This time is no different.

At first, we weren't the sole occupants of the *ohana* property. There were two other fairly habitable dwellings. In one of these lived a true-bloodline Hawaiian, Kai, his wife, Lek, and their baby. Kai was a quiet, smiling, prize-winning sand surfer, and Lek was from Thailand. In another dwelling lived David, a lanky Jewish man who played some mean beach volleyball. His parents were born in India and had emigrated to Israel. Somewhere along the way he had drifted over to Hawaii and set his anchor.

We also had a mystery neighbor that the kids nicknamed Thomas. He would occasionally emerge from a tall thick patch of buffalo grass and trees, driving a pickup laden with a rattling cargo of fishing poles and empty beverage cans. We didn't know, and we never dared ask, if there was a house back there. Sometimes it's best to just live and let live.

Most of our neighbors were warm and welcoming. I enjoyed practicing my Thai, learned during my years in Thailand, with Lek. David warmed up when Sharon invited him to come by the house and give an educational presentation to the kids about his home country. He also gave us a primer in beach volleyball. Over time, he began to call us Mamma Bear, Papa Bear, and Baby Bears.

Eventually, due to crossroads in their lives, each of these individuals moved on, and we became the sole occupants and caretakers of the house and grounds. As a momento of our various neighbors, I have kept a hefty framing hammer, given to me by David on the day he moved out. "I'm leaving the island Papa Bear, and here is a hammer for you."

THE COLONIZING FINGERS OF THE JUNGLE

Because the footprint of the property was over two acres, it required a lot of muscle and sweat to keep the jungle at arm's length. Although the jungle was a benevolent provider of privacy, we also found him to be a greedy colonizer. It became like a chess match between us. Armed with axes, shovels, machetes, mowers, and chainsaws, we hacked at the jungle daily only to barely keep up with his moves and countermoves.

First, he would send out his pawns—the notorious wide-bladed buffalo grass that grew into mammoth bush-like clumps. After these pawns had claimed a forward outpost, the "trash" trees such as haole koa and African tulip, were dispatched to consolidate the jungle's gains. Their coming signaled a near irreversible occupation.

The king piece of the chess match was a colossal rubber tree. Nothing on the property was taller or broader. From its far-reaching, sap-laden branches, the rubber tree sent down reverse roots to worm their way into the soil. These burgeoned into tree-trunk sized support columns until the rubber tree threatened to become its own sovereign, claiming a rival province measuring 139 feet in circumference. To ensure fealty, the jungle sent out the vines, snaking their way in and around, up and down, and between the king piece and its fellow trees. Checkmate!

Along with the nuisance trees, there were the good and lovely trees of the tropics, each giving us their own unique gift. "Dad, do you have some rope? We wanna make a rope swing!" the kids asked as they eyed a lofty monkeypod tree.

Aaron and Lucas make believe in the monkeypod tree

I analysed the prospects. With sturdy limbs and a trunk measuring thirty feet in circumference, it looked doable. "Why not?" I smiled. A day later, "AA-EEE-AA-EEE-AA-EEE-AA-EEE-AA," rang repeatedly and joyfully through the air.

Clusters of cheerful coconut and banana trees were sprinkled around the property, which rained down gifts galore. Using a reciprocating saw, I skipped the traditional machete method and buzzed the top off of a coconut. The kids snick-

Aaron and Katherine harvesting bananas

ered as they passed around the jungle mug and sipped fresh coconut water. Reverting to the machete method, I let each kid take a swing at the base of a banana tree to bring its fruit cluster to the ground (each stalk produces but once). We also hauled in buckets of avocado, lilikoi, lychee, and grapefruit.

The oranges in our jungle were more gag than gift. Some-

Aaron, Katherine, and Isaac harvesting coconuts

where along the way, their mother trees must have cross-bred with something burning and evil. "Yuck," Isaac puckered and squinted as he spit out a bitter bite of orange, "Probably what battery acid tastes like!"

THE TWO MOST MEMORABLE TREES

There were two fruit trees that were extra memorable, one fondly—and one not so fondly. On the fond side, the giant tree outside our kitchen door produced the golden fruit of the gods—plump, sweet Haden mangoes! There were so many during the bumper years that we did everything possible not to waste them. We dried and froze them. We made smoothies and jams from them and hosted mango feeds with our friends. One year we even put up a sign at the top of the lane advertising mangoes for sale, which had the added benefit of giving the kids some practice in salesmanship. In later years, when there were less children to feed, we realized the best way to handle a bumper crop was to share the aloha and give it away.

Harvesting mangoes had another useful byproduct: it cultivated family resourcefulness and

Haden mango harvest

teamwork. The fruit on the low branches was easy for the kids to harvest from step ladders, but the fruit on the higher branches was beyond reach. One day I huddled the team and presented some things I had collected from the salvage pile (useful items gleaned while demolishing the old houses). "Guys, does anyone see a solution here to our mango picking problem?"

In no time flat, a fishnet, a twelve-foot copper pipe, and two bolts had morphed into a respectable fruit picker. With the boost of a step ladder, it gave us, literally, the upper hand. However, the fruit on the highest branches was still out of reach. Accustomed to the perils of harvesting food (and vexed by its waste), I shimmied into the treetops and peered down through the branches. Pairs of up-stretched hands were nervously poised to perform the "soft catch."

"Keep your eye on the mango," I coached Isaac and Eric. "When it hits your palms, close your fingers and allow your arms to relax downward to soften the impact."

I heard mostly cheers of, "Snagged it!" interspersed with the occasional, "Oops!" followed by a thud. The catch-to-thud ratio was about 10:1—good enough for the minor leagues!

HAWAIIAN LOKI

Opposite in character of the benevolent mango tree was the sadistic jabong tree lurking in our side yard. Flaunting a massive trunk and a towering Afro of spiked branches, it assumed the role of Loki—the Norse god of mischief—in Hawaiian tree form. His steely thorns that pricked our skin when we pruned his Afro testified of his fetish for pranking us. Even Loki's jabongs (giant teardrop-shaped grapefruits) were an uncivil joke. Although the fruit inside was lovely and pink, eating it was an assault on our tastebuds.

Loki had other tricks up his sleeve. On one of our first nights in the Jungle Patch, he lobbed a jabong down onto the metal roof of the house. Hearing the crash, my sound-asleep body lurched awake.

"INCOMING," I mentally gasped.

"Andy, whaat waas thaat?" Sharon exclaimed.

My thoughts raced about how to save her and the kids but, eerily, I didn't know what I was saving them from. Then there was the telling sound of some object wobbling down the roof—whump, whump, whump! One second of logic later, I deduced it was the joker at work. The family was safe, and I would deal with Loki and his ja"bombs" in the morning.

To nix his ja"bomb" pranks, I chainsawed the branches overhanging the roof. Sweating kids frowned at Loki (and me) as they dragged the prickly limbs off to a mulch pile. But the

Jordan succumbs to Loki ja "bombs"

problem of the branches over the driveway remained. In a cunning act of self-preservation, Loki had woven those into knots with overhead powerlines. Anyone parking or walking below could wind up in Loki's crosshairs without notice—as Lucas' guitar teacher, Michael, found out. After finishing a lesson, he was floored when he went outside and found a ja"bomb" crater at the center of his shattered windshield. I could imagine Loki cackling, "Bullseye!" Although we had posted a "No Parking" sign on his trunk, Loki had deviously concealed the sign with some sprouting lower branches. Thus, we offered to foot the bill for Loki's sorry little windshield caper.

That's when I vowed to really stand up to our prankster. My strategic countermove was to create a ja"bomb" shield. I enlisted Lucas and Aaron to help me install two worn out trampoline mats over the driveway directly below Loki. We anchored these between Loki, the house, and the surrounding trees with ropes and bungee cords. When the first jabong plopped harmlessly into the shield's embrace, Lucas and Aaron gave each other proud high fives.

The celebrating was short-lived. When Sharon came home from work that day, I heard a yelp. "Andy, why are there two giant spider webs hanging in front of our house?" A more fashionable solution came when I met Mario, a strapping tree trimmer raising side-job Christmas money. He scampered up Loki, skirting the power lines using a body harness and rope tricks, and buzzed off Loki's Afro. With the the ja"bomb" threat squelched, the nets were decommissioned. Sharon cheered. At last we had reached detente with Loki.

THE KAUAI CHOP SUEY ROBBER

All trees and other things considered, the Jungle Patch was a fascinating stage, hosting many strange plays of events over the years. Of those plays, none was more bizarre than the Kauai Chop Suey Robber. It happened in the quiet of the night when Sharon awakened me, "Andy something's going on outside." Blue lights were flashing through the bedroom window. I saw several police cars parked in the driveway when I went outside to investigate. Officers were scouting through the jungle, shining their flashlights into the treetops.

To rule out sleep delirium, I approached a policeman and cleared my throat, "Is there a problem, officer?"

His blunt answer hit my ears like a bee sting, "We're on a manhunt." He further explained that their suspect had snatched the cash register from Kauai Chop Suey, looted the cash, ditched the register in the stream, fled on foot, and was possibly hiding in our jungle. I went back inside, checked on the kids, and locked every lock and jalousie lever I could find. After the police cars left, Sharon and I faded off to sleep.

The next day at breakfast, I said to the kids, "Strange doings in the Jungle Patch last night. There was a manhunt outside the house—and you guys slept through it!"

"No ways, what happened?" asked Lucas.

I told them about the robbery at Kauai Chop Suey and our visit from policemen. With all eyes fixed on me, I skimmed newspaper highlights of what happened after the cops left. "Says here that while the police were searching the crime scene, the robber snuck into a car and sped off. Then a brave officer reached through the window to nab him and got dragged for 50 feet." The kids' eyes grew wider as I continued, "The officer was ejected—luckily with only scuffs. A high-speed chase followed leading to a roadblock out on Kipu Road. The robber then veered off on a muddy sugar cane road and got stuck. He fled on foot but was soon tackled by a very tough cop. After a muddy wrestling match, the robber was wearing cuffs."

"Book 'em Danno!" chimed in Sharon from the next room, quoting Hawaii's famous TV crime show from the 1960s.

KID COMMENTS

Eric (11/28)

I loved the trees everywhere. I felt like I lived in a jungle. There were grapefruits, bananas, coconuts, lychee, lilikoi, and sour oranges. *All kine stuff fo' grind.* I would explore the back area a lot and find cool things.

A visit from our bovine neighbors

Lucas (9/26)

Life in the the Jungle Patch was one fraught with the unknown—excitement and adventure that would typically accompany a pack of boys being unleashed into *Jumanji*. There was behind every leaf, a strange creature; nestled high in every banyan tree, a new fort; through the harrowing itch of buffalo grass, an interesting artifact of previous inhabitants. My brother, Aaron, and I were determined to be the masters of this stretch of jungle we called home. With loyal cat in tow, we trekked far and wide across what seemed to be a jungle deep as any in the Amazon. We mapped our kingdom from the Lost Woods, around the Worm Tree, up Bum Hill, and all the way to the still unnamed northern reaches where we encountered a *Sandlot*-proportioned dog and promptly decided to respect his lines of demarcation.

Jordan (2/19)

There were other memorable features, including the long, slightly curving and bumpy dirt lane that led down to our jungle house. After so many years of riding up and down the lane, I think we actually memorized nearly every bump and divot. Another feature that gave our backyard a somewhat ominous feel were the two abandoned houses nearby. Years of relentless jungle advancement caused them to be overrun and infested with insects, plants, and vines of every kind. They were a vigilant reminder of why it was necessary to do my yard work each and every day to avoid the same fate befalling our house. As the old saying goes, "home is where the heart is," my home is one where there's a jungle outside, thriving with fruit, animals, and fun.

CHAPTER SEVEN

Raising Jungle Patch Kids

Isaac is chewing madly through a cluster of stubborn buffalo grass with the weedwhacker. A machete-wielding Eric is thinning areca palm branches. Lucas is raking leaves, and Katherine is gathering fallen branches. I smile. This is legit farm boy training a la jungle. I scan for Aaron and Jordan, hoping they are not being slackers. They are. Jordan is wearing a bicycle helmet and sitting in an old rusty wheelbarrow being pushed by Aaron. They are on a distant planet of play. I smile again. Though they are slacking, this is horseplay that makes work fun. This is one of my future gifts to them—knowing how to work hard and then to play hard.

Our rustic surroundings posed some lifestyle kinks indeed. But with those challenges came a unique opportunity for us as parents to both enjoy and mentor our kids. Sometimes I found myself giggling inwardly at the spectacle unfolding. There we were, living with six imaginative minds to entertain and shape, a jungle to tend to, and a tropical island to master. On the other hand, there remained societal conventions: careers and responsible financial planning, blah, blah, blah. Added to that was my ongoing inner conflict. I worried about being true to my resolution to quit gypsyness. I still wanted the kids to have continuity in school and for Sharon to have a log home in Bear Lake. But the debate was settled (or at least postponed) each morning when Sharon and I woke up with a certain anxious anticipation: how to best enjoy and channel the mix of energy and spontaneity swirling about us in our funky Jungle Patch.

To channel this mix, we fell back on the simple goal we'd always had for the kids: train them for their upcoming adult responsibilities, and have as much fun as possible doing it (so they wouldn't hate us for it later). Sharon and I divided this goal roughly in half. She was to be in charge of academics and would transition Study Abroad Kauai into the one-room tightly-run Jungle Patch School (JPS). I put myself in charge of work-ethic training.

To help me in my duties, I partnered up with two old-school trainers of my own creation. The first was prim Madam Housework whose program centered in indoor tidiness. The second was hard-boiled Madam Yardwork. Her program consisted of constant toil in snipping back the colonizing fingers of the jungle.

PASSING ON A LEGACY

My philosophy on work had been kiln-fired in the gritty and sometimes perilous world of farming and ranching. My summer jobs as a teen consisted of bucking hay, hoeing beans, and moving sprinkler pipes through calf-deep mud amid swarms of gnats. And I had studied the work ethic of my mother. When I was age ten, she and my father parted ways. Yet as a single parent, she remained determined to keep her self-reliance. Borrowing from her background of growing up on a thriving Illinois farm in the 1940s, she feistily launched an enterprise of livestock production at the idled railroad shipping corrals near our home—an improbable feat in a men-dominated industry. This gave her sufficient means of providing for my siblings and me.

Whenever I had a teenage "allergic reaction" to work, my mother gave me healing antihistamines in her lecture, "Andrew, honest, hard work brings self-respect. *And it puts bread on the table.*" Then she booted me out the door to tend the livestock or work in the fields. My teenage brain was peeved at her gall, but in retrospect, I am grateful for her tough medicine. It helped me learn how to put bread on the table. Now, it was up to me to pass this legacy on to my own children.

THE DAILY REGIMEN

The daily regimen of Madam Housework began from the moment the kids woke up. Sleepy eyes surveyed the dreaded whiteboard roster hung near the kitchen to check their room assignments for the day.

"Yesss," whispered Katherine, "porches—easy!"

"Ugh, kitchen—the worst!" mumbled Eric.

All of the assignments on the whiteboard—kitchen, bathrooms, living room, porches, and special projects—were rotated daily. It was expected that each child would keep their room organized and swept or vacuumed until the lights went out. It wasn't uncommon to see Aaron half-heartedly twirling a toilet brush, or to hear Isaac pleading with Jordan to keep his Legos picked up in the living room. Sharon and I chuckled at the irony of imposing the same "torture" our parents had "inflicted" on us.

The kitchen was the most dreaded assignment, probably because we did not have an automatic dishwasher. Not surprisingly, our kitchen managers were stingy in how many dishes were set out at dinner time. "No, everyone does not need a butter knife. We can all share the one," a miserly Eric often decreed.

Kitchen duty also meant disposing of dry and wet rubbish—a bit problematic because Kauai County was unable to make our stop (no safe turnout for their trucks). That meant storing two weeks' worth of dry rubbish in one of the old sheds and then hauling it to the transfer station.

"Who wants to go on a fun little expedition with Daddy?" I would invite.

"And where might we be going?" came a wary reply.

"To the dump!" Silence.

Appealing to the whiteboard roster, I announced, "Okay, Lucas, you're on special projects today. Let's go haul rubbish."

PAVLOV'S THEORY A LA JUNGLE

For wet kitchen rubbish, we developed an eco-friendly disposal system: a large bowl kept on the counter designated as chicken scraps. Once a day, the kitchen crew dumped the bowl far out in the jungle. The scraps were summarily devoured by the two dozen or so wild chickens that roamed the property. This system was smart for several reasons. On the practical side, it solved our problem of not having an in-sink garbage disposal. It was also a symbolic lesson about recycling to preserve Mother Earth. On the more genius side, the system taught real-time science and led us to discover the Jungle Patch Theory of Association:

Pavlov's Theory of Association	Jungle Patch Theory of Association
Control group: Hungry dogs Signal instrument: Bell Associated with: Food Effect: Mass canine salivation	Control group: Jungle chickens Signal instrument: Creaking screen door Associated with: Kitchen scraps Effect: Rushing, squawking poultry mob

Madam Housework piggy-backed conservation with other chores like doing laundry—the old fashioned way. Although we did own a washing machine, we never owned a clothes dryer. At first, we intended to buy one, but then an epiphany struck: what a shame it would be to waste the plethora of free green energy that was ours—solar and kid power.

My clarion call, "clothes in the washer," propelled the kids into action. Pencils dropped, trampoline flips ceased, Nintendo games paused, and Lego forts were abandoned. All kids without a doctor's note flew to the washing machine, emptied out the drum, and hung up an overflowing basket of laundry on a crisscrossing web of lines. I braced for habitual grumbling.

Socks were the most hated. "This is our third load today," mumbled Aaron as he flung a sock on the line.

"Socks are the worst! If I had a dollar for every sock I've hung up," added Isaac.

"Why don't we buy a dryer?" Aaron complained.

"Dad, Eric is just petting the cats," whined Lucas.

"Am not."

"Are too."

Then something changed. "Go, web, go!" yelled little

Clothes in the washer!

Katherine. She threw a sock to Aaron like Spiderman releasing his web.

"Up, up, and away web," commanded Aaron as he flipped his wrist to let a sock fly. What? Did I just hear laughter amidst the grueling servitude of laundry? Time had suddenly rewound to a more innocent bygone era as I watched my youngsters hang out "Spiderman" laundry to dry in the pure golden rays of the Hawaiian sun.

TAMING THE JUNGLE

Madam Housework was a decent, apprentice-level trainer. She gave the kids a gentle taste of community responsibility and sanitation, the elementary terms of adulthood. But to climb to advanced levels—determination and grit—a tough master sergeant was needed: Madam Yardwork. And while no teacher elicited more grumbling among the ranks than she, likewise no teacher elicited greater character growth. To pass her training meant graduating from a boot camp of sweat-and-grime labor.

Boot camp commenced with battling our nemesis—giant clumps of prickly, spiny, buffalo grass. When we moved to the Jungle Patch, hordes of these invaders had occupied the two open fields intended as play yards and pest barriers. Some of the clumps stood greater than six feet in height. Our family campaign to eradicate them took muscle, teamwork, and time.

"Aaron, pull harder," urged Lucas as he chopped at the exposed roots with a shovel.

"I am!" countered Aaron as he twisted the tops of the blades together and tugged with his might to wrestle the clump out of the ground. After ten minutes of toil, they succeeded in uprooting their pesky foe. Next to them, Isaac and Eric were fighting similar battles. Meanwhile, Katherine and Jordan did their best to tow the smaller clumps off to a mulch pile. After the fields had been reclaimed, the older children were to keep them mowed, and all were charged to keep a vigilant watch for buffalo grass infiltrators.

The mission then became a constant trimming back of the jungle's fingernails—making sure he respected the line we had

Katherine eradicating buffalo grass infiltrators

drawn in Kauai's red dirt. This meant weed whacking, trimming branches, and disposing of fallen limbs and trees at the perimeter of the open fields. Particularly important was the trimming of trees rimming the lane from the highway down to our house. Several times while attempting to exit, the jungle gave us a back-peddling uh-oh: a fallen tree or a one-foot diameter branch blocking the lane. It was either stay home or chainsaw our way through.

Most limb falls we handled in-house, but for safety's sake, some required experienced help. Luckily, I found a reliable backup—a rugged, common-sense local who called himself Native Rambler. One day I anxiously dialed his number, "Nate, I've got trouble. A monkeypod is blocking the lane and pinning down the power line."

"Rajah that! I'll grab my saw and be right over." A savvy tree-trimmer, he got us out of our logjam.

LEAF STORMS AND LEAF TACOS

In places where we shut the jungle down, he plotted revenge. In a perpetual pout, he spat out thousands of pounds of leaves over the years onto the open fields. This year-round leaf storm was new to us. Whereas leaf raking in Idaho had been a once-a-year autumn festival (rake the leaves into a pile and then play in it), leaf raking in Hawaii never stopped—ever. The toil of carting the jungle's leaves off to mulch piles gave the kids a clever idea.

"What's this?" I asked Lucas and Aaron who were raking leaves onto a huge tarp.

"Dad, wheelbarrows are junk for hauling leaves. This tarp can haul ten times as much." I admired their ingenuity as they folded the tarp over the leaves and marched toward the mulch pile. Presto, one jumbo jungle taco to go!

*Aaron, Katherine, and Lucas "happily" raking
by decree of Madam Yardwork*

While leaf tacos fast-tracked jungle cleanup, their abundant contents added to a bigger problem—two proliferating piles of mulch measuring as much as ten feet from base to summit. The footprints of these mini mountains had swelled ever outward because of the extra oomph needed to throw leaves and branches to the top. To keep the piles from taking over the Jungle Patch, I borrowed an analogy from Hawaii geography. "Guys, our mulch piles have become Big Island size. They're spreading like Kilauea's lava over the property. Let's shrink 'em to Lanai size. Aim for the top of the pile, 'kay?"

In later years after Madam Yardwork's students had graduated with high marks from her program, I awarded her emeritus status. I became sole caretaker of the Jungle Patch. One day, with Sharon as my witness, I did an experiment to quantify how many leaves fell per day from a single tree.

My control group was the Haden mango tree. After a cleanup in the evening, the ground around it was completely bare of leaves. In the morning, I counted the freshly-fallen

Aaron and Jordan playing yardwork hooky

leaves. "Honey, are you seeing this?" I called her to the porch. "There are 89 new leaves on the ground!" Using my phone's calculator I did a quick calculation and involuntarily blurted out, "89 x 365 days = 32,485 LEAVES PER YEAR. Argh!!! And that's from one tree among hundreds in the Jungle Patch." She smiled and left me ranting.

Soon thereafter, I devised the most clever method of all to deal with leaf storms, even surpassing the famed leaf-taco method. Using a mulching lawnmower, I shredded the leaves into little pieces down into the parent soil from whence they came. It's called the mow method, and it worked marvelously!

KID COMMENTS

Isaac (13/30)

Yard work was 70% of my childhood. We hacked at buffalo grass. We hacked at tree limbs. We hacked at weird tropical plants. We hacked and we hacked and we hacked and still the jungle forces advanced like Sauron's forces pouring out of Mordor. There were many times I cursed photosynthesis and every other biochemical reaction that could support such an ecosystem. But the hacking taught perseverance and working hard, and I can say the work ethic instilled in me by the jungle denizens are responsible for at least 70% of my current success.

Eric (11/28)

Different room every day. I am doing this to my kids. Although porch day was the best. You could get by doing nothing . . . hahaha.

Lucas (School Essay, age 14)

My brothers, sister, and I are all assigned different rooms of the house to clean. Every day we rotate to the next room in the order from kitchen to living room to porch to special projects to library and back porch all the way back to the kitchen again. Throughout the day we have to clean our room or we get a hefty penalty of 35 pushups or more! Another throughout-the-day responsibility is the hanging up and the folding of clothes. Our dad also assigns us our daily exercises: 50 push ups, 80 sit ups, and five sets of ten pull ups.

Aaron (School Essay, age 9)

The Worst Day!

First I woke up. Then we had to do skills and respect. That lasted for two hours. Then we did school. School took one hour. Then we hung up a white load, then we cleaned our rooms. Then we raked leaves. Then dad got mad at Jordan because he was crying. Then dad sent Lucas in time-out 'cause he made Jordan cry. Then we loaded up garbage. Then we moved the couch. Then we hung up another white load. Then we went to sleep and that's the end of the worst day ever.

Katherine (4/21)

I remember the day I learned how to sweep. My brother, Eric, was my teacher. As I think back on it, maybe he was doing it out of love, but it was most likely out of eagerness to have someone else handle the chore. "Pretend you're painting the floor," he told me. "Cover every inch of it in invisible paint." Because I wanted to be an artist when I grew up, I became a thorough sweeper from that moment on. This was in stark contrast to my other brother, Aaron's, "Elvis Sweep" tactic. There were two steps to it: (1) Twirl a rag across the table to get all of the junk off, then sweep that junk under the table and counters in a motion that resembled Elvis playing the guitar. Painting was fun, but I prefered the Elvis Sweep . . . until I realized it just made for more work later on deep cleaning days.

Jordan (2/19)

Another tactic to lessen the intensity of the work was to simply (when not in Dad's view) plop down on the most comfortable nearby clump of leaves or grass and talk story with our yard work partner (which throughout the years for me was usually my sister). The topic of such conversations were more often than not how mean Dad was for making us do yard work.

CHAPTER EIGHT

Education in the Jungle Patch

Sharon is working today. As her vice principal, and designated substitute teacher, I am in charge of school. (Yikes.)

"Okay, if we all agree not to tell Mom, we'll skip math (my weak suit) and focus on global geopolitics (my good-enough suit)."

"What's that Daddy?" asks nine-year-old Jordan.

"Err . . . geography." Pointing at our huge world map on the wall, I drill the kids in national capitals. "Germany," I open my oral quiz.

"Berlin!" comes the reply.

I try a stumper, "Honolulu."

"Not a country. Capital of Hawaii!"

I reach deeper, "Brunei."

"Bandar Seri Begawan!" Katherine trumpets.

"Nicely done," I nod and smile a smile of congratulations— and of personal accomplishment. Whether the kids ever go to Brunei or not is irrelevant; at least they are becoming mindful of their great big world and her beautiful peoples.

Whenever homeschool came up in conversations with new acquaintances, there seemed to be an occasional raised eyebrow. What were our motives? Were we anti-establishment? Did we allow our kids to eat candy? Truthfully, it was never our intent to protest anything or isolate the children in a jungle work colony (and, yes, candy was allowed). Quite the contrary. We wanted them to grow up with a healthy self-esteem, patriotism, a solid formal education, and a vision of going out in the world to make a difference. Initially, our decision to form the Jungle Patch School was simply about keeping our family's autonomy during our season in the sun. But as time marched on, we found homeschool to be a good fit for our family, and we continued on.

I don't recommend homeschool to anyone unless they are fully prepared to bear its daunting responsibility—and its unintended consequences. The daunting responsibility is that it became entirely up to us to budget sufficient time and resources to steer our children's vision of their future. We also had to ensure each child would be emotionally, physically, and academically prepared to seek an advanced education or vocational training. The unintended consequence was that we now wore a double task master's hat. Instead of just suffering the inherent hated role of harping, "Please keep your room picked up," we now bore the additional role of harping, "Please do your math and English assignments."

Thankfully, Sharon was naturally suited to handle this responsibility and its unintended consequences. She had a love for formal education and was eager to pay it forward to our children. She was also, by nature, miraculously even-tempered. That said, the early years were rough around the edges, but as she refined our homeschool, the JPS became a respectable academic institution. As she built it, she learned to graciously thank well-meaning family and friends who sometimes probed how our children would gain socialization skills and, most importantly, how they would gain entry into college. (More on how everything worked out fine in *her* version of *Lost in Hawaii, Book Two*.)

SKILLS AND RESPECT

While Sharon's talents elected her to be the JPS schoolmaster, my MO of up-and-at-it nominated me as its PE coach. In the early months, my program was a no-frills workout of calisthenics which ended in a pull-up challenge. We also did a baseball drill where I tossed up pop flies in rapid succession to the older four, one by one. The exercise ended as soon as each rookie caught all their pop flies in a row.

I proudly announced to the kids one morning, "PE is now known as Skills and Respect. You will enhance your motor skills, develop a tougher psyche, respect your mentors, and become fit as a fiddle." They, however, viewed the program differently and coined their own cynical term for it. Each morning, I proclaimed, "Skills and respect everybody!" One day, I heard Isaac mutter under his breath, "You mean *gutties*, right?"

The disclosure of this snide nickname made me realize my boring program needed a facelift. Scanning for ideas, I had an epiphany: a mere four blocks from our house was a tropical

"Skills & Respect"

beach equipped with volleyball courts. Hello! Why not make volleyball our PE and the chipper opening of our day? Thus began our family's love of beach volleyball. At first, however, it was anything but romance. Our clumsy matches often veered into water polo realms as we chased shank after shank into the ocean.

COACHING METHODOLOGY

In coaching JPS athletes, I had several role models to follow from my sports years at Valley High in Eden, Idaho. Everyone in this country school (my graduating class was 40 strong) got to play sports if they wanted to. Some of the coaches were patient and cerebral; others were more loud and reactive. The coach I admired most was our varsity football coach, Forrest Fonnesbeck. Somehow he made us feel more powerful than we actually were—drive eclipsed size. At age 16, I was 5'6" tall and weighed 138 pounds (suited up) when he said to me, "Stennett, you're now one of my defensive ends. When the other guys hike the ball, don't let ANYTHING outside you—even if it's 180 pounds and six foot tall." Though he showed patience in leading us, he was also relentless and tough. If we slacked off, we did tedious drills and ran wind sprints until our attitudes were properly adjusted.

As JPS coach, I found myself emulating the Fonnesbeck model the most. I admit that the glaring hot sun and my own version of wind sprints gained me much *stink eye* from JPS athletes. But volleyball, to me, wasn't about honing a physical skill—it was a series of object lessons simulating life's demands that would soon fall on their adult shoulders. One day they would have to take initiative, work as a team, and never give up—in spite of the wearisome heat of adversity.

Years of daily volleyball have etched vivid memories in my

mind. Even now, I can picture every detail of a typical volley-ball morning.

It is about 8:20 a.m. Sharon, Katherine, and Jordan are strolling Kalapaki beach looking for shells. For the oldest four, JPS volleyball is in session. On a sand court, warmed by the morning sun, I drill bump-set-spike with my athletes. The court is bordered by the inviting lawn of a luxury resort on one side and tempting surf on the other. But we aren't here to relax. In the bump circle, I call my young recruits to attention, "Okay, Isaac and Eric, pair up. You'll stand Lucas, Aaron, and me." We hustle into position.

"Zero, zero service," Isaac calls out. He sends a fast-flying serve. It clears the net, bearing hard toward Lucas.

"Move your feet!" I bark. Bespeckled Lucas is tottering backwards trying to catch up with the ball's velocity. Too late. The ball glances off his outstretched fingertips, and his body plows backwards into the sand. The ball careens onto the lawn, where an amused tourist grabs it and hands it to a pursuing Aaron. Lucas has just completed the foul-up known as the tip-over.

On another serve, Aaron lazily extends a flailing arm and a clenched fist to defend. The ball shanks wide and rolls into the ocean. He has just completed the can-of-juice foul-up.

Everyone braces themselves for what comes after a cluster of foul-ups and a soaked volleyball. "Everyone take a lap around the keiki palm tree!" Then, I give THE LECTURE. "Children, the first thing that moves in volleyball is your feet. You must get ahead of the ball and into stance in time to receive it!" An hour has passed and I call out, "Let's do our laps." We then end JPS PE with a refreshing plunge into the surf and a lap along the crescent-shaped shoreline.

As a coach/father, I do have some regrets. I would've, could've, should've been much more patient and less bossy in my training sessions. I fear that the lessons of life I so nobly intended to impart—refusing to mentally drag one's feet in life, and thus, get ahead of the trials life serves you—were often weakened by my strictness. On the bright side, however, I like to think that the kids' many years of Kalapaki digging, setting, spiking—and moving their feet—have contributed to their success and independence as adults. Also on the bright side, through practice and time, the tip-over and can-of-juice blunders became extinct and gave way to a truly enjoyable game of near majestic skill.

Over the years Team Jungle Patch welcomed many walk-ons. During evening pickup games there were the temporaries—guests from the hotel or the cruise ship who invited themselves in. Some played an advanced game. Others seemed to be using fencing or batting techniques (we were never sure). The tipsy ones half-irritated and half-entertained us with their playbook of jolly lunging swipes and tip-overs. And then there were the morning regulars like the kids' friends from Kapaa: Adrienne, Danny, and Kaylee Hale (also homeschool-

Team Jungle Patch in training

Team Jungle Patch trained

ers). Another walk-on was homeschooler Jesse Sherrill, one of Aaron's friends. At first, Jesse pouted at his compulsory attendance and played horribly (he was the inventor of *can-of-juice*). His "mean" mom had insisted he play beach volleyball with his friends every morning. But as he matured emotionally—and grew really tall—he became a champion player.

Another memorable walk-on was a gentleman named Pat Cassier, enjoying an extended winter stay from New Hampshire. One morning he walked up to me wearing his great big New England smile. "I've been watching your family. It's terrific. I was wondering if my grandson, Jared, and I could join you?" That led to a wonderful friendship between our families.

One last walk-on was a moped-riding beach loafer named Eddie. His promising future on Team Jungle Patch imploded suddenly one morning when he exclaimed, "Gotta go guys!" and bolted from the court for his moped. We were deeply puzzled by his mid-match exit, until we noticed hotel security swooping in. They told us Eddie had been banished from the hotel property for sketchy doings.

Team Jungle Patch and walk-ons, Hales and Cassiers

SENSEI SAM AND TAEKWONDO

The Jungle Patch School was a dynamic organism for teaching. Whenever an opportunity knocked, we quickly opened the door. One example was a young college grad from the mainland named Sam who showed up on Kauai to visit his sister. Sam was Mr. Spontaneous and had studied abroad in Japan. He was also a Taekwondo black belt. He seemed to be in no particular hurry to leave Kauai, so I floated a deal to him, "Sam, how 'bout you hang on Kauai until your future plans gel? You give our family Taekwondo and Japanese lessons, and we'll give you room and board."

"Okay, let's do it."

For six months he stayed in the old house next door. His living room became a dojo. Outside the dojo we were his friends, but inside we were his students. Five days a week we removed our flip-flops, entered the dojo, and bowed. We stretched out until we heard the stern command from Sam, "Chari-yut." We quickly lined up in a row as he called out, "Attention stance." I glanced sideways at the row of eager students. At the far end was Sharon (being a really good sport). In between us were all of our kids except three-year-old Jordan— off in a netherworld of couch play. Following Sam's command, we straightened our legs until they were barely touching each other and pointed our toes forward.

"Katherine, Eric, stiffen your arms," Sam belted out. "Fighting stance." We turned our bodies to the side to make ourselves into smaller targets and bent our knees for balance. We raised our hands to protect our heads and shifted our weight to our back legs. We focused on perfecting our form as the tempo of Sam's commands increased, "Jab, punch, uppercut, crane, front kick, crescent kick, ax kick." Sam was relentless. "Isaac, an uppercut is delivered with full force. It's not a cheer." "Sharon, you can't punch someone if your thumbs are sticking out like that." After drills, we sparred as the sweat poured from our faces.

Eric sparring with Sensei Sam

"Watch it, Eric, " I gloated as I flipped him to the ground.

"You were saying," he said as he did a surprise leg sweep which sent me staggering.

After a full hour of thrashing, Sam called Japanese class to order. "Well done, or as the Japanese say, *Yokudekimashita*!" I'm proud that you have all gotten *hiragana* down pretty good, and we'll continue to work on a some *kanji*. But today I want to introduce the *katakana* alphabet, used to spell foreign words."

"Huhh . . . now why did they have to go and make three alphabets when one is good enough?!" Isaac cynically protested.

The day came that Sam heard another call and moved on. The empty dojo evolved into a lonely storage closet for our stuff. But each time we entered, we felt a tug to bow, as echoes of "*chari-yut*!" blinked to life in our memories.

THE JPS MUSIC PROGRAM

Besides Sam with his martial arts and Japanese, three musicians came knocking at the JPS door as well. One was Suki, a gushingly cheerful Japanese immigrant. She came to the Jungle Patch weekly and taught taiko drumming and piano to Aaron, Katherine, and Jordan. There was also strummer-man Michael, the guitar teacher (who fled the scene after Loki ja"bomb"ed his windshield). Perhaps the teacher that left the greatest mark was a tall, energetic blonde named J'Net that moved here from California (the "mean" mom who made Jesse play beach volleyball). She brought a lasting gift of violin music to the JPS, especially to Katherine. When J'Net helped her play her first tune of "Johnny Gets a Haircut," a flicker, and then a flaming fire of love for the violin, ignited within Katherine.

Admittedly at first, it was mildly painful to hear the screeching of a novice violinist in the house, practicing the same simple tunes time and again. I was fairly tolerant of it because I was the loving dad, but some of the siblings dreaded it. Eric dubbed her violin the "screech-o-lin" and sometimes hid it from her to end his misery.

As her talent blossomed and sweet notes began to flow from her strings, tolerance grew to appreciation. Eventually, I would even beg her to keep practicing so I could hear her soothing melodies. And oh, how I loved the reverie of her back-walk concerts! After a long day's work, I would lie face down on the couch, while Katherine (who has excellent balance) walked up and down my aching back and played her violin.

I gave her hints about the playlist, "How 'bout one of those snappy Irish fiddle tunes. Do you remember how to play any of those?"

"Of course, silly Daddy," as she launched into "Miss McLeod's Reel."

JPS "ACCREDITATION"

Sharon and I have often tried to put into perspective fourteen years of running our one-room Jungle Patch School. Was being both parents and teachers worth it? Was it a successful venture? All we can say for certain is that we had a lot of flexibility to make extraordinary family memories—many of which were made in homeschool itself. But there was also stress—especially for Sharon who bore the brunt of organizing and administering the curriculum. But after seeing the oldest four march to receive their diplomas at the university of their choice and then become gainfully employed (in computer domains), we would have to say, YES, it was worth it!

Lucas, a sample JPS university grad

And YES, it was successful! And when the last two complete their current majors and march across the stage, it will provide the final seal of accreditation for the JPS.

KID COMMENTS

Eric (School Newsletter, age 12)

PROTEST. The Stennett kids protest about the problem of doing exercises on spring break. "You look stupid if you don't," says campaign leader Eric Stennett. The campaign did not go well and is most likely to give up hope. We will see.

Katherine (4/21)

My mom always made sure homeschool was what we really wanted to do and that we had a choice. I remember one day she sat us all down and had us name off the pros and cons of going to public school. I loved watching shows like *The Lizzie McGuire Show*, where kids had lockers and backpacks and ate lunch in cafeterias. So when my mom asked me to name off the pros of going to public school, I named those things.

I remember her smiling when I said it would be "so cool" to have a backpack. But now that I have all of those things and more in college, I can fully appreciate the perks and life lessons of homeschool. It taught me many things, but I think the overarching lessons I learned were independence and self-control.

Needless to say, starting at Kauai Community College when I was sixteen was a bit of a learning curve. The GED was the first "real test" I had taken, and it terrified me. But doing well on it gave me the confidence I needed to start community college. The first day of school I wore my best everything: jeans, shirt, and new messenger bag. It was all a blur, suddenly living a life I'd only seen on TV: wondering where my classes were, responding to my name being called on the roll, and finally, classmates that weren't my brothers!

Katherine (School Essay, age 11)

Beads of sweat rolled down my neck as I waited impatiently for the server to serve on the other team. The glaring sun pierced my eyes, so that I couldn't see at all for a few seconds and the ball landed right in front of me as I took a dive into the sand. It covered my sweaty arms and legs, making it stick. Quickly I brushed it off and put myself unwillingly into a ball-receiving stance. The ball covered up the sun for a split second then came shooting down in between me and dad. "Go Katie!" he yelled, and I ran toward it and it hit my already red wrists making them sting with pain, but I forgot about it when the ball made a soft thump on the ground on the other side. A sign that showed we had won!

Jordan (2/19)

Because I have five older siblings, homeschool wasn't as lonely as one might think. In fact there was plenty of rowdy socialization, more so than might be expected of a school with a student body of six. Throughout the years I witnessed my siblings graduating one by one, leaving the house, and going off to college. As such, Jungle Patch High socialization dwindled down to my sister and me, and eventually to just me.

CHAPTER NINE

Jungle Patch Adventures–
Unplugged

*Early this morning I made three King Arthur swords out of
woodshop scraps and gave them to the kids. They were silly toys,
I thought . . . they'll probably never see action. How could they
compete with store-bought battery-operated light sabers? Later
in the afternoon, I am in for a surprise. Out in the baseball field,
I spy Lucas, Aaron, and Jordan wielding the wooden swords in
a mock duel of knights. With only room for two in the arena,
Jordan takes a knee as Lucas and Aaron fence for their spectators,
Jordan and Francis, the cat.*

Month after month and year after year breezed by without the Jungle Patch selling. It was as though this place
had summoned us from 3,000 miles away in Idaho to claim
us as its stewards. Admittedly, I was fairly romanced by the
castaway feel of it all. Calendars, clocks, and even time itself
dissolved into a blur. We had no cable TV, and we lived in a

Jungle Patch knights

Eric and Jordan improvising a Jungle Patch shelter

jungle! The beauty of this unplugged lifestyle is that it pushed the kids outside to entertain themselves. And though the jungle was their yard-work taskmaster, it was also their beloved friend, full of fun, surprises, wisdom, and improvisation.

One improvisation had to do with the wheeled, speedy things all children seem to love: skateboards and scooters. Eric was especially smitten with skateboarding. But there was an obvious problem—the one hundred percent lack of smooth concrete in the Jungle Patch. Creative thinking—fueled by Eric's burning need for speed—led to the design and construction of the Jungle Patch skate ramp. Born of scavenged plywood, boards, screws, and a father/son flurry of tools, our project was finally done.

"Watch this, Dad," Eric said as he climbed up to the launch point.

"Oh my, what did we build?" I whispered as Eric launched and raced towards me, jumping over a stack of boards he had placed at the end.

Eric on the Jungle Patch skate ramp

"Haha, that was awesome," he cackled. I breathed a sigh of relief (no broken bones—yet). "I'm gonna learn how to ollie and kickflip," he said. Knowing I didn't know what he was talking about, he YouTubed for me some pro skaters doing totally hazardous moves. Like I said, "Oh my, what did we build?"

BIRDIES AND RACQUETS

Another improvisation was the half-grass, half-dirt badminton court we carved out of the jungle. "Dad, got time for a game?" Jordan invited, clutching two racquets and a birdie. How could I refuse a teenage son who wanted to hang out with his dad?

"Zero to zero" he called. Swish came the birdie. I did what I thought was a maven move to the right and slammed the birdie back. Before I could congratulate myself, the birdie was zinging past my nose. "One to zero," he grinned. Apparently the days when Jordan fanned the air as birdies flew by were long gone.

I tried a little trash talk. "Boy, don't mess with me. You do know, don't you, I was badminton champ of my eighth-grade PE class?" (There were seventeen of us.) I returned his next serve. He hit the birdie high into the air, but it never came down.

"Aw man, it's in the branches again. Dad, can we please cut 'em off?" Using one of his flip-flops as a missile, he dislodged the birdie back to earth. Many lobs and slams later the final score was Jordan 21, Dad 18. Jordan gloated, "Who's badminton champ now?!"

Putting our rivalry aside, Jordan and I made a plucky team battling challengers who came to the Jungle Patch. One day, Braden Lindstrom, our friend and a teacher at Kauai Community College, phoned Sharon, "Hey, I've got some students I'd like your family to meet."

Sharon replied, "Sounds fun, tell me more."

"They're a young married couple from mainland China. Their names are John and Lisha, and they like badminton."

Sharon was intrigued. Having the kids learn firsthand from foreign visitors about their cultures was high on her homeschool wishlist and, so far, they had never met anyone from China. "Sure, bring them over," she said. Hanging up the phone she announced, "Guess who's coming over for a game of badminton?"

"Hello, hello," John said, flashing a smile that covered his face. "We are so happy to meet you."

"And we are so happy to meet you, too," I smiled back. After introductions, teams were selected, and badminton good times ensued. I knew that whichever team had tall, swift Braden with his eagle-width arm span would surely win. I was right, but it didn't matter to anyone who won. John laughed

Badminton with John and Lisha

at everything, including eating Braden smashes. On breaks, Lisha gravitated to the cats and chatted it up with Katherine. Later, over hot dogs and root beer, the kids were enthralled to hear all about China. "Where did you come from?"

"Chengdu and Nanjing," they answered.

"What kind of food do you like to eat?"

"Wontons are great, but this hot dog and root beer are sooo delicious!" John raved. (He had just downed his first American hot dog.)

This was the beginning of a lasting friendship, and I have kept, as a token of our amity, the pro-grade rackets they left for Jordan and me when they left the island.

THE TRAMPOLINE ESCAPE

At center stage of Jungle Patch fun was the gravity-free circus of the trampoline. Aaron and Lucas entered this circus frequently, taking turns as audience and acrobat. When one ripped a mad stunt and landed it, the other belted out a belly full of laughter and gave it a ridiculous label. "Bahaha, the 'Hablaitzen' maneuver, do it again!" Then they switched places and launched incrementally higher into their anti-gravity galaxy.

There was always time for a trampoline sideshow. It would happen in the day, in the night, and even in the pouring rain. The rat-a-tat of a cloudburst on our metal roof delivered a telegram below that critical mass had been achieved for an aquatic barrel-rolling air show, and out the door they flew.

Of all the kids who reveled in this circus, Jordan seemed to crave it the most. His habitual solo acts, however, centered less on exhibition and more on personal escape. Jammed by the tedium of study, he would disappear out the door, whereupon we heard the creaking of the trampoline springs and the soft "pow, pow" of battle sound effects. His aerial skills were second to none, but he spent most of his time skipping and hopping round and round the perimeter of the jumping mat

Trampoline daydreams

in his sun-splashed bubble of jungle. Watching him from the big picture window, Sharon and I noticed that his lips moved steadily as he seemed to be conversing with an invisible friend.

After a jump session, he often cornered Sharon or me and uploaded the entire contents of his brain. As it turned out, his conversations on the trampoline weren't conversations at all, but mental blueprints of wild inventions he was envisioning. Sharon saw the value in his ideas and one day handed him a notebook to record his epiphanies. "Better start securing patents," she chuckled, "And you might want to think about how to schmooze hall passes from your college professors for trampoline breaks." Who knows—one radical idea in that notebook might someday change the world.

THE SKETCHY CHILI COOKOFF

Jungle Patch playtime was as lightly supervised as possible. Not hovering was a welcome reprieve for both child and parent, but there were risks. In one incident, a visiting friend, Anthony, fell out of the rubber tree and broke his leg. In another chancy incident, I found myself following an extension cord leading from inside the porch down into the crawl space beneath the house. I had not put that cord there; the question was who had, and why? I followed the mystery cord to its subfloor connection: an old, rusty microwave oven. In front of the oven were some ragged couch cushions. I investigated and found that Lucas and Aaron had looted the said oven from one of the abandoned houses, snuck some cans of chili from our kitchen, and planned to have a chili cook off. Huh??? Were we not feeding them enough?

I hastily broke up the cook off. "What's going on here? That oven is an ancient rust bucket likely to electrocute you, and it's a petri dish of germs under there!" Now armed with hindsight (and the memory of their crestfallen looks), I wish I could somehow rewind and redo. I would have tried to patiently teach instead of issuing edicts to get immediate results. After all, they were boys having fun (and in an odd way being resourceful) in their subfloor hideout.

KID COMMENTS

Lucas (9/26)

If we were to rule, we would need a castle to keep all the parents, girls, and pests out. We finally settled on a sturdy mango tree overlooking the emerald sea of the cattle field as our sanctuary. With a bit of wood, nails, and rope, we crafted what could only be described as a lost boy's home. The most memorable structure was a simple platform of wooden planks between two branches that extended over the fence into the field. The sway of the tree and the lazy Hawaiian sun filtering through the canopy there facilitated much needed rest after a hard day's exploration. One of our biggest finds was a grave-yard of rusted cars that the jungle was heartily tucking away. We crawled through the undergrowth and rotting wrecks, collecting keys until we were the proud owners of a fleet of unrecognizable cars and one VW Bug.

Aaron (7/24)

So we went searching through the scrap piles created from the demolition of the old houses. One thing that caught our eyes was an old microwave. We thought it would be a cool addition so we promptly carried it to our base under the house. After we'd placed it, we started thinking it would be rather awesome if we actually cooked something in it. So, we went into the house, retrieved a few cans of chili, and then connected the microwave to an outlet. Unfortunately our dreams of cooking under the house were very short-lived.

Jordan (School Essay, age 9)

One time I was sitting around playing Nintendo. Then I heard the truck come in which was my dad. I went out to hug him. Then I noticed a big box on the back of the truck. Then I went up to see what it was. It was a big trampoline! Then my dad and one of my brothers helped him unload it. They brought it over by the lychee tree and assembled it. The first ones on were Lucas and Aaron, then last, me and Katherine. I had so much fun that I almost jump on it every day.

Jordan (2/19)

The trampoline for me was a portal to another world or more accurately, worlds. After the first bounce or two, the surrounding mango tree, jungle, house, brawling cats, and meandering chickens would all disappear. Then all that was before me were colonial foot soldiers brawling with orcs that were being barraged by a nearby necromancer that had raised an army of the dead.

CHAPTER TEN

Kauai Aesop's Fables: The Jungle Cats

I am gazing out the living room picture window at Lucas and Aaron. They are sitting surprisingly still on the trampoline mat. Their bouncing party has given way to a different kind of party. Six feral cats have leaped up to extend a paw of friendship to their jungle neighbors. Lucas and Aaron reciprocate by stroking their fur and tickling their tummies. I recall my own boyhood experience with animals. It was rather bipolar. On the one hand, I cursed milking bossy cows and fleeing for my life from reeking billy goats. But on the other hand, I savored riding a lightning-swift mare named Sally and the deep friendship I shared with a cowdog named Raccoon. No matter the case, I am grateful for the laughter, the lessons learned, and even the drama from being around animals. Now I am glad that my own children are getting at least a small taste of these gifts through their feline friends.

One of the most delightful surprises the jungle produced was the dozens of stray cats that wandered into our lives and into the children's hearts. They came in different colors and sizes, but they had one thing in common: they were hungry for food and affection. Adopting these migrants had many benefits. First, they were effective soldiers in our rodent extermination squad. Second, caring for the cats taught the kids

Pile of Jungle Patch cats

how to nurture living things. Lastly, we got to see ourselves in the mirror by watching the real-time Aesop's fable happening outside our doorstep: "Jungle Patch Cats." There was always a moral to be learned.

ZELDA AND JUDGING

One cat that Jordan rescued from starvation was a scrawny, crooked-tailed kitty known as Zelda. By putting out meat scraps for Zelda, Jordan whispered her into docility. Watching Zelda eat by herself one day, Jordan observed, "Dad, have you noticed how Zelda gets super cranky when the other cats come near her? Even the nice cats she hates."

"Well, the jungle is full of

Zelda, the loner

some pretty scary stuff for an orphaned kitten. She's probably a bit scarred," I offered.

THE BUFFY COMPROMISE

Not long after the taming of Zelda, another kitty appeared on the kitchen window sill while we were eating dinner. Its heart-melting meow evoked a squeal from Katherine, "A kitty!" She bolted out the door followed by her brothers. Scooping up the ball of fluff in her arms, she announced, "I'm going to name her Buffy."

"It's Lhoates," challenged Aaron with one of his more exotic random names.

"Hmm . . . a good second name, but kitty's first name shall be Buffy." I settled the matter in her favor (who sometimes lost out by virtue of her being outnumbered five to one).

THE INVICTUS MRS. DUDE

As if we didn't have enough jungle strays, there were the kittens Katherine dragged home one day. She found them at the side of Menehune Fish Pond Road, four tiny helpless siblings about to be run over. Scooping them up and cradling them in her arms, Katherine brought them home and, through pleading eyes, begged, "Daddy can we pleeease keep them?"

I weighed my

The invictus Mrs. Dude

response carefully. Saying yes meant instant hero status, lasting for at least a good month. No meant plummeting to villain status; I couldn't bear the thought. "Okay, but only if you agree to be their mamma!"

These kittens had gentle dispositions, unlike many of the skittish jungle strays. The most remarkable of the four was Mrs. Dude. When she was young, an infection turned her right rear leg into a stiff, dragging appendage. Because she walked with the gait of a pirate, the kids affectionately dubbed her Peg Leg. Down but not defeated, Peg Leg compensated by developing buff shoulders and front legs. (She looked like a feline bodybuilder.) This allowed her to hunt rodents and defend herself handily.

TIGER THE BULLY AND NEEDLES THE PEACE-MAKER

At times we had ten or more cats that called our porch and feeding tray home. When the population was high, tensions ran high, and object lessons abounded. One big tomcat, Tiger, seemed infected by raving jealousy. He was friendly to all humans and loved their affection, but after getting it, he went on a tear of picking fights with the other cats. It was as if he was warning them, "Don't go seeking affection from the humans 'cause it's all mine."

Tiger's opposite was an old, handicapped cat named Needles. Her presence seemed to evoke calm within our family of cats. Unfortunately, the day came when Needles, the matriarch, died, and unity among the cats began to unravel. Splinter groups and hissy fits became rampant. I took this moment to say a little something to the kids. "Guys, as you grow older, you'll notice that people and cats are a lot alike. For whatever reason, perhaps personal troubles or insecurities, a few are gonna want to pick fights and put others down."

"Tiger!" Aaron interjected.

"Uh-huh," I continued, "But there are lots of other people who are kind and giving. Some even have a special way of making peace—like gentle old Needles. Which would you rather be?"

A SOLUTION TO ALL THINGS

Although fond of our cats, we kept them outdoors where they were free to roam the jungle. But this made feeding them problematic. One day, ten-year-old Jordan, lodged a complaint, "Dad, when I feed the cats, the chickens charge in and eat all the food, and the cats don't do anything to stop them. I'm tired of standing guard. I've got other things to do!" This was a catch-22 because the chickens were our most important allies as bug eradicators but were now acting as pests.

Putting our heads together, we rigged up a chicken-proof feeding station—a roomy plywood cage with open sides cov-

Chilled out kittens in the cat feeder

ered by chicken wire. The cage was elevated off the ground by corner posts. Atop was a snappy red roof. A cat-sized hole was cut into the bottom of the cage with a cat ladder extending down from the edge of the hole. Now, cats—but not chickens—could ascend and feed as they pleased. Jordan could now cross "guard duty" off of his very busy to-do list.

IT'S OKAY TO GRIEVE

There were so many cats that came and went from our lives that it was hard to keep track of them all. To cherish their memory, Isaac, in a homeschool art project (or doodling brainstorm), sketched out a feline family tree, sorting out our cats' family lines. On the tree was a mix of names that ranged from *Star Wars* characters like Qui-Gon, to Pokemon characters such as Pikachu. As with all pets, there were inevitable moments of sadness. While the birth of kittens was a celebration of life, the death of a cat was distressing. Whenever a cat was lost in action, we helped the children dry their tears and say aloha by holding a memorial service and burial in its jungle home.

KID COMMENTS

Jordan (2/19)

Our cats were forbidden by our parents to be in the house (since they weren't necessarily the cleanest of animals). However, when Mom and Dad weren't present, that rule was somehow conveniently forgotten and we had some fun cat parties in the living room from time to time. Some of the smarter cats also learned how to invite themselves in by squeezing their little paw into the gap around the screen door and prying it open. That would lead to a wild panicky cat chase with stuff getting knocked over until they found their way back out.

CHAPTER ELEVEN

Kauai Adventure:
The Jungle Patch Guide

We all inch our chairs closer to the crackling campfire—not only because the air is damp and chilly, but we are roasting marshmallows to make s'mores. Behind us is our big tent and dining canopy set up with a cooking station. In the moonlight, the silhouettes of mammoth redwoods sway gently in the breeze. It is a lovely setting for our family's two-night stay in the mountains of Kokee. As a dad/protector, I am happy knowing that all the dangerous stuff is far away, down in the ocean. There are no bears, big cats, or snakes here in Hawaii. I am also happy that there is no cellular service, which means no screens or social media. We are forced to rely on an ancient method of socializing—talking to each other without texting!

Beyond the backyard fun of the Jungle Patch, Kauai's world-famous beaches, mountains, and waterfalls begged to be discovered. Like a storybook filled with legendary settings, Kauai called out to us to become her guest characters. Some of the finest chapters were the unsung excursions within a ten-minute radius of the Jungle Patch. The bike ride to Ninini Point was one of these. Tires aired up and chains lubed, we pedaled up our bumpy lane.

"Not fair!" Lucas complained. "Why do Kates and Jordan get to ride in the bike trailer?"

"Be humble, no grumble," I quoted a local saying.

Not far from the entrance to our lane and across the highway, we entered the winding promenade leading to a luxury hotel. Our rough and tumble ride transitioned into a smooth glide amidst manicured groundcover and flowers. Above us was a cooling canopy of leafy monkeypod limbs. We imagined this was an extension of our jungle lane. "My, the gardeners are doing a fabulous job here, couldn't we get them to work a little harder down by the house?" Sharon joked.

Riding on, Isaac hollered, "There he is, there's Brutus." Brutus was the nickname Aaron gave to the massive white statue of a toga-clad Adonis leading a raring Roman stallion. There were actually eight Brutus statues—one anchoring each corner of two classical bridges that arched across the shimmering lagoons. "Hey Brutus. Aloha Brutus," the kids saluted as

Bike riding the promenade

we passed Brutus after Brutus. (The statues were stunning, but we forever wondered what they had to do with Hawaii.)

Threading through the golf course greenery beneath fluttering palms, our ride waned into a rough gravel road. Alien sounds erupted in the bike trailer behind me. Katherine and Jordan used the road's washboard texture to distort their jabbering voices. Soon we pedaled into the friendly shadow of the golden-yellow lighthouse of Ninini Point. The kids bailed off their bikes and skittered into the vast obstacle course of black boulders sloping down to the ocean. "Playing tag! Not it!" Eric called out to start the first impromptu game.

Several cement platforms overlooked the boulder fields— reserved front-row seating to enjoy the "boulder games" and sideshows. Each jaunt to Ninini promised something new. "Thar she blows!" Isaac bellowed, spotting breaching humpbacks on winter vacation from Alaskan waters. Sometimes, tugboats chugged by, towing freight barges to and from Nawiliwili Harbor.

Pointing to a cruise ship, Katherine pleaded, "Daddy, can we please go on one of those?" There was also the entertainment of watching the ocean's mood spectrum. Soft white overspray on her black boulder boundaries meant she was all chilled out. Heaving overspray signaled she was in high spirits.

Topping things off was a gutsy air show: low-flying airliners and sometimes National Guard fighter jets used the lighthouse to guide them to touchdown at the adjacent airport. Lying supine on the lighthouse's cement apron, we beheld illusions of aerial wizardry as daredevils tagged the bellies of their craft on the lighthouse's crown.

Ninini Lighthouse airshow

JAUNTS TO AHUKINI PIER

The extended version of Ninini was to bike the airport's coastal road to Ahukini Pier. This dirt "road" was basically two deep vehicle ruts, which after heavy rains, filled up with stagnating rainwater. Buffalo grass flanking the roadsides slurped up the abundant moisture and swelled into six-foot-tall, inwardly-drooping sidewalls. In the center of the ruts and walls was a perilous narrow hump. Biking in caboose position on a jaunt with Jordan and his friend, John, I watched a blur of pedaling pandemonium. As buffalo grass fiends clawed at their arms and faces, they yelped and zigged pell mell across the hump to the opposite rut—only to be sideswiped by fiends on the other side. Next came a wobbling, panicked zag— again, to meet the same fate.

Building a survival hut at "Pocket" Beach

Fifteen minutes of zigzagging later, we came to a welcome retreat, an unnamed pocket beach. The piles of driftwood lining the shore sparked my imagination. Picking up a long piece of driftwood I hinted, "Wow, we could build a fort with this stuff." An hour later, lost in the moment, Jordan and John had made decent castaway huts. Extricating himself from the sand beneath his low-lying hut, Jordan imitated, in a mock British accent, a famous TV survivalist, "Uh, I'm here on Kauai in a bit of a tight spot trying to get myself out of this here cave."

Soon we came to our journey's end, Ahukini Pier, Kauai's main harbor of old. We sauntered over its sprawling grid of eroding concrete walkways. Being a John Wayne fan, I quizzed them, "Do you guys know which John Wayne movie was filmed here?"

"Dad, who is John Wayne?"

Ughh!

As the kids grew older, their interest in Ninini biking waned. Katherine, however, still enjoyed it. Eyes fixed on the azure horizon and sitting on the old cement platform next to

Ahukini bike ride with Hale and Schumacher friends

Ninini poetry session with Katherine

me, she opened up about her dreams, and recited her on-the-spot nature poems. "The clouds up high are cute and fluffy, almost as cute as my little Buffy."

A MOUNTAINTOP RESTAURANT

Handily located within a seven-mile radius of the Jungle Patch above Kapaa Town was another old-reliable outing: trekking Sleeping Giant. Legend states that this mountain is a behemoth who ate too much, fell asleep, and is yet to awaken. On Jordan's tenth birthday, he announced, "I wanna hike the Giant."

It happened to be one of those days in paradise—a pleasant 70-something degrees with a few drifting clouds and a gentle trade breeze. With light hearts, we entered the regal corridor of Norfolk pines marking the trailhead on the *mauka* side. Onward and upward, we passed through groves of strawberry guava trees. I plucked a handful of guavas and handed them out. "How cool is this?! A natural sweet-and-sour energy snack." Trekking on, I snuck ahead, scuttled up a tree and, from an overhanging branch, staged an ambush. As my fellow hikers passed below I growled, "Raaaar!"

Aaron rolled his eyes, "Daaad." Not the rise I was looking for.

Luckily, I had a second chance—Sharon was coming up. "Raaaar," I growled in my best bear voice.

"Ahhh," she jerked her shoulders, "ANDREW." (I have learned that "ANDREW" is a signal to lay low.)

At the summit, we broke out our footlong sandwiches and savored the commanding 360-degree view of the eastern shore, the Wailua River, Kapaa Town, and the central mountains. "Wow, it's like we're in a world-class mountaintop restaurant!" Sharon chimed in.

This reminded me of our one and only such experience— eating a fancy salmon dish atop Sun Valley's elite Bald Mountain. "Yeah, and a fair bit cheaper!" I quipped.

While sitting on our rock chairs, Katherine said some-

Jordan and Katherine enjoy Sleeping Giant's mountain-top restaurant

Aaron, Andy, and Jordan at the summit of Sleeping Giant

thing so kind and beyond her years that it became etched in my heart. As the sunlight cast a gleam on Jordan's ocean-blue eyes, she complimented her birthday-boy brother, "Your eyes are so pretty."

I almost choked up fumbling for the pause button. I wanted to linger forever in the symphony now playing: the perfect weather, the pleasant scenery, the endorphins of the hike, and most of all, the beauty of family friendship.

ROOFTOP OF THE ISLAND

Widening our radius to forty miles from the Jungle Patch, along the island's southern coastal road, we found Kokee State Park. At 3,500 feet above sea level, this mountainland—enshrouded in ferns and forests, sunshine and mist, daytime warmth and nighttime nip—jolted our senses from the lull of lazy lowland beaches. Gouging its way through this upland is the fabled Waimea Canyon.

Our base camp here was often the employee cabin provided by Wilcox Hospital, a plantation-era house surrounded by rolling manicured lawns bounded by an outer ring of thick woods. Enjoying evening cabin ambience, we binged on Sharon's yummy food, tons of snacks, Monopoly, Scrabble, and a silly game called Loot. In the daytime we rushed headlong into treks (dubbed death marches by cynics) and mountain biking.

THE ALAKAI SWAMP

Perhaps the most memorable of all our Kokee treks were those through Alakai, the world's highest swamp—a weird world of thick hedgerows and waist-deep mud bogs. Fortunately, much of the 3.5-mile trail is covered by boardwalks. During one hike with Isaac, Eric, Lucas, and some of their friends, the Alakai played a wild card and cloaked itself in fog and drizzling rain.

Trekking Alakai Swamp

"This is the worst," complained a drenched, shivering Isaac.

"Who knew we were suppose to bring boots and a parka," Eric added as he slugged through the mud in his flip-flops.

I secretly agreed but tried to put on a brave face. "One foot in front of the other guys. Keep moving and you'll feel warmer. And before you know it, we'll be there." Finally, peering through the wispy veil of clouds at the lookout, we spied sun-drenched Hanalei Bay far below.

"Please, oh please, beam me down Scotty!" cracked a near-hypothermic Lucas.

PEDALING WISDOM

Kokee bike rides not only supplied good times, but hidden life lessons, as well. One day fourteen-year-old Katherine and I rode from our family camp by the meadow up to the Kalalau Lookout. I knew the two-mile ascent would be tough, but I figured it would build her confidence (and mine). Descending and ascending the road's saddles, I glanced back now and again to check on her. Eyes fixed on the road ahead and pedaling hard, she seemed determined. When I crested the summit, I paused to savor the victory. All that remained was a short downhill coast to the lookout's parking lot. I glanced back to cheer Katherine on. She was dejectedly walking her bike. When she caught up, she scolded herself. "I knew it, just when it was the last hill, I gave in."

I offered her a hand up. "Yeah, but look at what you did accomplish. Even though you walked part of the way, you still reached the top!" I knew that being surrounded by five brothers had prodded her to be a tough competitor, and my current pep talk was having little effect. But also a nature-lover, her

The "What are gears?" bike ride in Kokee with Jesse (far right)

mood was soothed as we coasted down to the lookout and took in the ethereal views of Kalalau Valley.

Another Kokee lesson happened when Jordan, Aaron, their friend, Jesse, and I biked the loop around the Boy Scout camp. I prepped the group, "Gang, it's gonna be smooth sailing on the downhill, but it's gonna get rough coming back up. Remember to gear down."

On one grueling upward push, I looked back to check on everyone. Aaron and Jordan were on my six, but Jesse was lagging way behind, so we stopped and waited for him. Finally he caught up, huffing and walking his bike. I was puzzled since Jesse was a fit, athletic kid.

I hinted, "Hey guys, what gear is your bike in?"

Aaron answered, "1:1." Ditto Jordan.

Jesse, sheepishly asked, "Uhh, what's a gear?" I then demonstrated what the shifters on his handlebars were and how to use them to make climbing hills much easier. Jesse was relieved. "Man, when I saw you guys climbing like wild men, I was freaking out that I was so out of shape!"

So much for assuming your clear instructions are clear.

SOMEWHERE OVER THE RAINBOW: KALALAU BEACH

Coming down from Kokee, and lying forty miles west of the Jungle Patch on the northern coastal road was an especially daunting chapter—the twenty-two-mile round-trip Kalalau Trail, which begins at Ke'e Beach and ends at Kalalau Beach. Relatively few people ever set foot on this mile-long, pristine beach, although many see it from boats and helicopters. Even if one is willing to pay the price in sweat and tears to get there, only a limited number of camping permits are issued per month for hikers or kayakers.

Our family's first taste of this trail was when Isaac, Eric, and I hiked it with their Boy Scout troop for a two-night stay. To make it easier for the younger scouts (and dads) we skipped the first eleven miles of the hike by boating to the edge of Kalalau Beach.

"Okay, everyone out," ordered the boat captain. We cast ourselves overboard and swam ashore along with our gear wrapped up in plastic bags. Greeting us was a gang of non-permit, "long-term campers" standing on the beach (some in near-native attire), who seemed oddly entertained by the swimming, chattering Boy Scouts.

Once everyone was out of the water and our gear was stowed, we began to explore the beach. On its upper border, we cooled our feet in a pool filled by a miniature waterfall trickling over a ledge of rocks. On the beach's far south end, we wandered into sea caves. Facing east, I snapped photo after photo of a towering backdrop of sculpted green *palis* resembling cathedral steeples. On an evening sunset stroll, Isaac exclaimed, "Look guys, a perfect sunrise shell!" He scooped up the bright orange and yellow treasure and put it in his pocket. "Dad, won't Mom be excited? It'll be the coolest shell in her collection!"

In the heart of our camp, the aroma of frying fish mingling with salt air and campfire smoke teased our appetites. Steve (my old night diving pal) had speared some fish using his speargun and dive gear (which he regretted bringing later when he had to freight them out). Meanwhile men and boys, many of them fathers and sons, rough-housed on the warm sand and in the brisk surf. On the first night, Isaac, Eric and I slept in our tent under a patch of trees away from the beach. As I nestled into my sand-padded tent-floor mattress, I began to hum in my mind a certain rebooted song now popular in Hawaii. To my tent mates I said, "Guys, don't you think Kalalau is the place described in those song lyrics, *somewhere over the rainbow?*"

"Dad, it's so hot," came the replies.

Feeling pushed off of my sentimental cloud, I jousted back, "Oh, so sorry, I forgot to bring the fans and portable generator."

On the second night, we opted to sleep on, rather than in, the tent, using it as a ground cloth on the high side of the beach. The breeze from the waves cooled us, and Kalalau's ceiling of twinkling stars sung us a soothing lullaby.

At 7:00 the next morning, we marshalled the troops to begin the onerous trek out. Those who packed light were glad, and those who had packed "luxuries" began to hastily donate them to the locals. Unfortunately, a few of the boys came down with a fever and had zero energy to walk out. Eric was one of them.

"Son, can you make it out?" He gestured there was nothing else he could do. I gave him ibuprofen and helped farm out the sick boys' gear among the hiking party. Then we hauled

Jordan and Isaac enter Crawlers Ledge, Kalalau Trail

ourselves up the 600-foot rise of Red Hill. "One foot in front of the other," I coaxed Eric (and myself).

Soon we came to the infamous "Crawlers Ledge" between mile markers seven and eight. A few of us adults went first to prove the footing. All my senses came suddenly online. On my right was a rock face soaring above my head. On my left was another precipice, plummeting hundreds of feet below into the ocean. All that separated the two baleful inclines was a footpath measuring but a few feet across. Luckily, the footing was firm and the wind was subdued, and all made it across safe and sound.

Treading on, the mind-bending vistas of the Na Pali Coast summoned my camera lens at every new rise and bend. Meanwhile, the Keeper of Kalalau, the Hawaiian sun, rose to his zenith and levied his fee for admission—a nonstop offering of sweat from our brows as homage to this unearthly place. Our moxie began to wane. I kept a close eye on the water supply to make it last, giving the lion's share to Eric so he wouldn't become dehydrated. I suddenly recalled a bumper sticker I

Hanakapiai Beach

had seen: "I survived the Kalalau Trail." I chuckled to myself, "Uh-huh, I totally get it now."

Nine miles later, when the Hanakapiai Stream met my feet, I tossed my backpack on the shore and belly flopped into the cold, clear water. We had but two miles to go which gave a morale boost to Eric and the group. Finally, at around 6:00 p.m., our ragtag troopers had tromped to the trailhead and into the merciful arms of their moms. Now I just needed to go buy one of those bumper stickers.

KALALAU ABBREVIATED

It was never realistic to hike to Kalalau Beach with the entire family *and* have fully harmonious bonding. Fortunately, Kauai offered a compromise: the two-mile family trek to Hanakapiai Beach. Call it Kalalau Abbreviated. Here we got to challenge the same rugged Kalalau Trail while gawking at the same beautiful Na Pali Coast. We even got to enjoy the crescendo of winding up on an epic beach. The compromise was the slashing off of eighteen miles of walking (no one ever complained about this).

An especially memorable trek happened on this trail with seven-year-old Jordan. We had taken Sharon's brother and his wife, visiting from Santa Barbara, to get a gander at the Na Pali Coast. The plan was to hike to the one-mile marker, which offered a decent profile view of the coastline. Though it was late in the afternoon, a few of us determined there was just enough daylight left to hike the additional mile to Hanakapiai Stream and make it back to the trailhead before dark (we had no flashlights). Energetic Jordan wanted in, even though it meant hiking barefoot because a strap on one of his flip-flops had blown out on an earlier hike. The wives, on the other hand, wanted out and fell back to the trailhead. Squish, squish went Jordan's little bare feet on the trail's muddy sections; patter, patter on the dry. (A fair number of regulars do hike this trail barefoot.)

Soon we heard the telltale sound of babbling water—we had made it. Below the trails steep rim, we saw the welcome sight of Hanakapiai Stream coursing through the boulders and greeting the Pacific via the handshake of Hanakapiai Beach. After descending to the stream, we shot some quick photos and beat a hasty retreat out. I warily monitored the setting sun on the horizon. It was going to be close. Jordan was showing fatigue. "Come on my little man. You can do this. Daddy's sooo proud of you!"

As dusk approached, the wives grew concerned. Sharon related to me later that she asked some emerging hikers, "Excuse me, have you passed anyone along the way?"

They replied, "Yes, we saw some some men with a poor little boy who had no shoes hiking in the mud."

She feigned, "Wow, what parent would allow such a thing?"

All worked out well when, in the dim light, we happily beheld the faces of the wives and the trailhead markers. On the drive home, Jordan sank into a deep slumber and didn't wake up until the next day.

SWIMMING IN ICE WATER

On some of our other hikes to Hanakapiai Beach we tapped deeper energy reserves (and got an earlier start) and trekked upstream along the creek another two miles. Suddenly, there was Hanakapiai Falls, plunging from a 300-foot black cliff into a glorious swimming hole.

A local man cautioned me, "Watch out. Da water stay ice cold."

I thought smugly, "Cold water? Why, he knew nothing of cold water until he had swum in a snow-melt, Idaho mountain lake." Plunging in, I gasped for air. He was right, and I retreated swiftly to the shore, wearing a hangdog grin.

COOKIES ON A HOPPING BOAT

Our adventures on land were sprinkled with voyages by sea—some of which bordered on being misadventures. Lucas, Aaron, and I were the lucky recipients of promotional passes for a snorkeling and whale-watching tour. In high spirits, we sailed out of Port Allen on a large catamaran toward the Na Pali Coast. It was a day where imagination could not compete with reality. As the vessel cut through the choppy water, we were greeted on every side by Poseidon's friends.

"Dad, there are tons of dolphins racing the boat!" pointed Lucas.

"Dad, get a picture of that!" cried Aaron, pointing to a huge tail of a humpback whale slamming into the water.

We oohed, aahed, and laughed. An all-natural Sea World

show danced around us against the backdrop of the rugged green cliffs of the Na Pali Coast. An hour later, we anchored atop a large underwater cavern near Lehua Rock. Donning snorkel masks, we splashed into the ocean to discover this giant rock's underwater secrets.

As we climbed back into the boat, I smiled as the underwater expedition was rehashed. "Did you see the schools of Needlefish?" said Lucas.

"Yeah, but the coolest ones were the Moorish Idols, I think that's what they're called," chattered Aaron.

The kids prattled on as they devoured hoagie sandwiches and chips. Soon the prattling stopped, and I knew why. As the captain rammed the boat high speed through the choppy Kaulakahi Channel back to port, it took ninja-level focus to keep our hoagies down. Somehow Aaron and I did, but poor Lucas didn't fare so well. He actually had things under control, and we were not far from port, when a bubbly attendant came through asking, "Cookies . . . anyone for cookies?"

Lucas, who has an acute sense of smell, braced himself for the unthinkable—that someone might take her up on her offer. Sure enough, the guy sitting next to Lucas spoke up, "Over here." He was a navy man and seemed proud of his sailor gut. The moment he opened the package—releasing the slightest whiff of cookie—Lucas was doomed. He shot to the front of the boat, groping for any open retching slot along the railing. Although the tour was awesome, we were never so glad to set foot on land as we were that day after the boat hopped and chopped its way back to port.

KID COMMENTS

Isaac (13/30)

I went with my dad and brother, Eric, to the Na Pali Coast

on a Boy Scout outing. This was like camping in the mountains back in Idaho but 90% more fun. Thirty percent of the extra fun came from riding in a boat to remote Kalalau Beach and throwing out waterproof bags containing our gear into the water and swimming to shore with them. Another 20% was provided by an awesome natural waterfall we used as a shower. The rest of the fun was provided by swimming on a beach that seemed like it was at the edge of the world and finding a rare "sunrise" shell, which I gave to my mom because I'm a good son. The only not-fun part of the trip was seeing a nude camper in all his glory doing yoga.

Aaron (7/24)

For one of my Boy Scout merit badges I needed to earn cycling. Dad and I went to the hot, dry west side of the island. Undaunted by the heat, we pedaled from Kekaha and entered the unpaved rocky road to Polihale Beach. By mid-point, our water bottles were empty, but we knew there was a drinking fountain at the end of the road. Upon arrival—much to our dismay—we discovered that the drinking fountains were not working. Parched and under the scorching sun we set off on the second half of our journey. Luckily we found liquid salvation in the vending machines at the seed company on the highway back to Kekaha.

Katherine (4/21)

Access to Ninini Lighthouse was on a red dirt road that snaked along the airport landing strip. It was gravelly and bumpy, and as I rode my bike, I would say my "A,B,C's" out loud because it made my voice rattle. There was a stretch of the road that was smooth red dirt, and I loved the sensation of gliding on it. Dad was usually ahead of me, and he would purposely swerve and make waves with his tires. I tried to entwine my tire design with his to create a sort of DNA pattern.

Then the ivory lighthouse towering through the azure sky guided us the rest of the way. But the real piece of heaven was sitting beside my dad on the slab of cement that overlooked a palette of lava rock boulders and crashing waves. We talked about the deep things of life, even when I was young. He'd take off one of his DC skating shoes and place it under his head, and I would lay my head on his outstretched arm. My ears filled with the symphony of the waves, wind, and his deep, knowing voice.

CHAPTER TWELVE

The Pest-War Misadventures

I am standing on the porch wondering what's up with Jordan. His eyes are bulging, and he is nearly hyperventilating to tell me something. He has just returned from dumping the big red kitchen scraps bowl into the jungle.

"Dad, I was walking back to the house when I heard a pig snorting in the bushes. Lucky I had my BB gun locked and loaded, 'cause I've seen a lot of 'em out there lately—and when I saw one chasing me, I took off running. Dad, it was just like in Mission Impossible. I twirled around and shot him, smack in the nose. The bugger went squealing into the bushes, and I never even dropped the bowl!"

I tease him a little, "Aww, are you sure you hit him in the nose, and was he really chasing you?"

"WELL, YEAH!"

"Very well then. I dub thee Jordan, Pig Slayer of the Jungle Patch."

Living in the raw world of the Jungle Patch gave us some eye-popping perspective about the food chain. It also gave us some survival-of-the-fittest misadventures (the kind you laugh about only after *many* years have passed). That's because there were a LOT of other life-forms competing for nutrition besides us *Homo sapiens*. In science books, these life-forms have polite Latin names and are sorted into a fancy classification system. For real-time clarity in the jungle, we bagged all that and made up our own system. With minor exceptions, non-*Homo sapien* life-forms were given one rude name, PEST, and were lumped into one classification, ENEMY COMBATANT. In other words, we were at war! (One side note: every house in Hawaii has pests to some degree, unless it is airtight, doused in pesticide, and surrounded by pavement.)

In recent years, I have suggested to my computer programmer sons to invent a videogame modeled after our pest wars. Although not a fan of videogames myself, I have always been amused at watching my kids hypnotically play them. Knowing I was annoying them, I would interrupt, "So what's the objective here?"

Jordan gave a hurried explanation once. "Dad, there's Link, and there's the boss. Link's the good guy. The boss is a monster who hates Link and wants to end him. When Link takes out that boss, he'll take on a bunch more next-level bosses. When the last mega-boss is down, Link wins."

Aha! That's when the plot for my pest-war videogame was born. Instead of Link, there would be Hawaiian Kimo wearing *slippahs* and a garish red aloha shirt. Various pests from mini to juggernaut would be the bosses that challenge Kimo for his jungle home. And thus it was in the Jungle Patch. We were all Kimo, living a daily videogame life battling pest-bosses to keep possession of our house.

The first line of defense in our war was establishing a perimeter shield to keep pests out of the house. This meant constantly patching cracks in the house's exterior, keeping drains covered, and window screens in good repair. Also guarding the perimeter was a legion of organic allies: the jungle cats who prowled for rodents and two dozen feral chickens that patrolled for bugs. Finally, inside the house itself was a backup: a gauntlet of traps posing as food sources. But some ultra-determined pests managed to breach both shield and gauntlet. When this happened, it meant resorting to fearsome hand-to-hand combat. Here is a taxonomy of the pest-bosses we dueled, as well as our strategies to avoid GAME OVER.

LEVEL 1: Wood Assassins

The most despised of the mini-bosses were the termites. Their angle in the game was to liquidate my wallet by slowly eating our house, piano, books, and anything composed of cellulose.

"Look, I vacuumed like five minutes ago, and here it is again," complained Sharon. She was pointing at a small mound of fine grains of sand under our bedroom door. "And there's more in the bathroom and the boys' bedroom."

I groaned, "Termites."

"Well, I don't see any," she responded.

"Honey, let's hope the day never comes that you do!"

Several nights later my hopeful wish for her was dashed. I heard screaming and ran into the living room where I saw several F4 tornados of drywood termites swirling around Sharon and the kids. Other F4's were raging in the kitchen and hall.

"Quick, grab every flyswatter you can find," I ordered.

Eight Kimos mounted a swatting counter attack. Outnumbered 1000:1, our efforts were futile, but in the battlefield blur, one plucky hero (not to brag, but it was me) had an idea that saved the day.

"Kill all the lights except in the living room. And bring me the vacuum!" I bellowed. The tornados swarmed the light. Hours later, the last termite was finally sucked into our strategic weapon. In the aftermath of the termite turf war I replaced the tattered plywood wall sheeting which had played host to this termite colony with non-wood sheeting.

RIP Wood Assassins. (Please don't take it personally—it was either us or you.)

Kimo 1, Pests 0.

LEVEL 2: Murky Shadows

Another mini-boss was the foul cockroach. They didn't lighten our wallets like the termites, but they did elicit horror with their helicoptering, scuttling, and popping up in unexpected places. Everyone hated them—especially Sharon.

"Eww, yuck—Eric, there's a giant cockroach in the shower—help!" she yelled from the bathroom. Eric grabbed a flyswatter. Slap, slap, slap, went the flyswatter as Eric knocked over the shampoo, shaving cream, and toilet bowl cleaner.

"Aha—got it!" Eric proudly announced. He scooped it up on the end of the swatter and dumped it in the toilet.

Sharon was relieved for the moment but worried about the next encounter. We bought roach traps and a dozen more brightly-colored flyswatters. The pink, blue, and yellow anti-roach weapons now hung in every room. Pointing to the gaudy new wall accents, I encouraged Sharon, "Look honey, we've invented a totally chic jungle-house decor." She faked a smile for me. In time, all became battle-hardened roach-swatting warriors. Even Sharon became a commando swatter-scooper-dumper of this vile mini-boss.

Kimo 2, Pests 0.

LEVEL 3: Blood Robbers

"Look, I'll give anyone twenty-five cents if you kill any indoor mosquito and bring me its carcass," I bribed the kids. I hated this stealthful mini-boss, who had the audacity to swoop in, steal our blood, and leave an itching red bump. I realized soon enough that at the rate we were going the promised bounty would soon break the bank; the body count was enormous. We needed to attack the root of the problem—the standing water where mosquitoes lay their eggs. I sent all kid Kimos on a mission to search out standing water and, where possible, empty it. This, plus indoctrinating all to keep screen doors closed, swung the battle in our favor.

Kimo 3, Pests 0.

LEVEL 4: Armored Wriggler

The tempo of the game was ratcheting up rapidly. Next in line was the ultra-speedy, ultra-scary super-boss centipede, whose bite packed a wallop of pain. Considered a delicacy by our wild chicken allies, less than ten of these ever squeaked past the shield and into the house during our seventeen years. But when one did, a dark and heated duel—requiring cool heads—ensued.

"Throw a book on it," yelled Isaac as a five-inch centipede scurried across the living room. Plop went the dictionary onto its crush-proof, armored body.

"I think we got it," said Lucas."

Someone get a bowl," Isaac yelled.

"Got it," Eric said in a full gait from the kitchen. "Everyone ready for the capture?" All heads nodded.

"Okay, release the beast," Isaac ordered. Lucas complied and lifted the book, while Eric slammed down the bowl to trap the fleeing centipede. I chipped in and brought the last piece of hardware for this attack move: a special flat metal sheet. Sliding it under both the centipede and the bowl, we completed OHC (Operation Humane Capture). From there the boss was taken outside to duel with its own bosses, the chickens.

Farewell Armored Wriggler. You were a worthy foe.

Kimo 4, Pests 0.

LEVEL 5: Ghastly Phantom

This next-level super-boss delivered a spike of shock and awe like none other. The cane spider, with its five-inch leg span, was like a phantom. It seemed to materialize out of thin air in the shower, on towels, and on the walls. We knew they were not venomous, but still, who wants to be face-to-face with a tarantula-like spider? The first sightings found us ill-prepared and poorly armed. We grabbed magazines and even a pan and swiped wildly—hitting nothing but air and upended furniture.

With the coming of fly swatters in every room, it became much easier to exterminate this boss. (Surprisingly they crumple into a tiny dot with a well aimed flick of the wrist.) Their mercurial speed did require backup. One Kimo was designated as the attacker. If he missed or lost his nerve, all backups present played tag-team.

Kimo 5, Pests 0.

LEVEL 6: Tusked Woofer

Despite our solid victories through level five, we remained vexingly stuck (to this day), on Level 6 battling the juggernaut boss, the razorback hogs of the jungle.

"What's that noise?" Eric shuddered one night. "It sounds like the velociraptors in Jurassic Park."

"No, it's just pigs," I said glumly.

My mind flashed back to my boyhood. Raising swine had educated me concerning their uncouth manners of uprooting

Tusked Woofer bosses

Woofer boss down

everything in their path. And I had not forgotten the terror I felt while fleeing to the top of a fencepost with an offended sow in pursuit. Snapping to, I realized the mess and the danger we were in. Mobs of razorbacks were now invading from the nearby stream bed, uprooting vast swaths of our lawn with their bazooka snouts. Their tussles over mangoes produced squeals of savagery and pain that shattered the serenity of the night.

"Get the BB guns, and let us do our worst," I said. We exited the house and crept as close as we dared. "Fire at will," I whispered.

We heard a few muted squeals as the herd scattered. "Ha, take that," Eric taunted. Fifteen minutes later, they were back noisily sparring, munching, and slurping.

Hmm. . . to take out this boss would require outsourcing. We networked with friends and friends of friends—anyone with hunting or trapping skills. One day, Robert, a bow-hunter, came to our rescue. He sat in our carport and downed eight pigs in less than an hour. The kids, in awe, dubbed him Legolas. It was a win-win. We got rid of the pigs (for a while), and he shared the meat with his family and friends. Legolas notwithstanding, months later we were back at ground zero. It was not unlike battling the Greek Hydra: cut off one head and two more grew in its place.

Kimo 5 ½, Pests ½.

And so, after playing the Pest Wars video game for seventeen years, we, a troop of hardy Kimos, have learned the tricks to avoid GAME OVER. And we can state that we remain triumphantly—yet tentatively—in control of the Jungle Patch. (Note to my programmer sons: I want a cut because I thought of it.)

KID COMMENTS

Eric (11/28)

I hated cane spiders. Cockroaches are fine. Geckos are fine. Centipedes are not that bad. Cane spiders in the shower or toilet . . . I hate that. That's all I have to say about that.

Aaron (7/24)

Walking down the lane to the house at night was scary enough, but the pigs didn't make it any better. I heard branches snap, leaves rustle, and alien-like sounds. It seemed like I was in a real-life horror movie. Even though I knew (at least I think I did) what was out there, the noises never failed to transform my timid walk into a quick sprint to the house.

Katherine (4/21)

The Jungle Patch gave me nerves of steel. While most girls' first reaction is to scream at the sight of a bug, mine is to grab a shoe and kill it. I wasn't always that way though. The sight of any spider used to send me running for my brothers or Dad. Cane spiders were the only ghosts that ever roamed our house. We rarely saw them, but they would pop up when you least expected it—sometimes in the roll of toilet paper, other times on my bedroom wall. Though I knew their fate lied in the quick flick of a fly swatter, their long legs made them appear so much scarier than they actually were.

CHAPTER THIRTEEN

How We Made a Living: Rooster Humor and Golf Balls

"Toss another corn chip," I nudge Lucas. Seemingly from out of thin air, flocks of wild chickens from all directions are beelining toward our family picnic in the Kokee meadow. All the kids have caught on to the game and are tossing out sandwich bits to stir the frenzy of the mob surrounding us. I begin snapping pictures of roosters sporting flamboyant tail feathers and noble hens nurturing up to eight fluffy chicks. "Throw more crumbs," I nudge again, in order to keep our squawking friends close. There are two key photos I capture—a proud running rooster in front of a lava boulder and a sweet mother hen minding her delicate chicks— that will forever change the way I make my living. They would become the genesis of Rooster Humor.

All parents have to decide where they wish to raise their family—Anchorage to Zurich. And they must decide what they are going to do—Accountant to Zookeeper—to provide for their family. In the grand alphabet of options, my decisions defined me as "KC." I live on Kauai, and I am a card designer by profession. How I came to be a card designer is as happenstance as our winding up on Kauai.

I have always envied people who knew exactly what they wanted to do, who did it, and who found career contentment.

It was never that way for me. Deciding what to do to provide for my family was always an unstable and humbling battle that stretched back to my roots in Eden. Topped with nomadic forays to the Sun Valley mountains, I was superbly happy in this bucolic world.

One day my mother said to me, "Andrew, I won a bid to harvest lodgepole pines up Warm Springs Canyon in Ketchum."

"Awesome, when do we start?" I exclaimed. (Lumberjacking was on my bucket list.) For several weekends, we toppled trees and dragged them by our horse, Old Chief, to the stock trailer and hauled them home. There, I made the poles into a beautiful stockade corral. Yup, all I needed was a highboy 4x4 pickup, a blue heeler to ride in the back, and a sturdy pair of leather boots and gloves.

But mentors steered me otherwise, "Boy, your body can't last forever. And someday you'll have to provide for a family. Get an education." I did so and landed a career as an analyst for the federal government. But sitting at my desk in suburban Maryland, I longed for the endorphins of physical labor in the untamed outdoors. I chided myself for craving such simplicity, but after accepting that I wasn't happy in my legitimate—but sedentary—career, I resigned and headed West to find myself. There I entered a wrenching career identity crisis: white or blue collar—which was it to be?

It turned out to be a compromise. I started my own business (white-collar) and resumed the trade (blue-collar) I had done to earn my way through college. That trade was garage doors. As unglamorous as it might seem, my business offered a surprisingly hefty benefit package. First, my office was the unconfined, fresh air of the Mountain West and a brawny diesel pickup fitted with an arsenal of power tools. Second, while other dads waved goodbye to their kids in the morning and went off to work, I often took a few of mine with me. Third, my only boss was the customer I got to please, and I got to feel rewarded by the craftsmanship I had rendered. Fourth, I got to scamper up and down ladders, lift, bend, and stretch at will. (It saved mega bucks on gym fees!) Lastly, was the scenery. I often caught myself transfixed inside a garage by the sight of living paintings: wild mountain scenes displayed in a mini-IMAX garage door opening.

Fast forward to Kauai. As our season in the sun began evolving into a life in the sun, I had to reckon with the leviathan of providing for six kids in a state with one of the highest costs of living in the entire country. I also had it on my radar to secure a modest security for Sharon and me after the kids were gone. The island harassed me daily, "So what is your financial plan young man?

A DIFFERENT KIND OF POULTRY BUSINESS

To answer that question, Sharon continued to secure cash flow and health insurance through her part-time nursing. She also began squirreling away some retirement funds. That was a big relief for me as I continued my career search and to dabble in garage doors. Meanwhile, through much trial and error, I launched a wholesale souvenir business called Rooster Humor. My product was a line of greeting cards, fridge magnets, hats, and T-shirts spoofing Kauai's feral chickens. The line catered to the Kauai tourist who begged to know, "Why, oh why, are there a gazillion wild chickens running amok and roosters everywhere crowing in my ears?" Through networking and pounding the pavement, I established thirty wholesale accounts with gift shops throughout the island. After getting Rooster Humor healthy and running, I exhaled. Finally, I had made a baby-step toward answering the island's challenge—and settling my career identity crisis.

TRIAL AND ERROR WINS OUT

The evolution of my card line was anything but a carefully mapped out capitalist venture. It was a lucky collision of the American Dream, a market niche, pent-up-energy, and personal hobbies. The hobbies were photographing mother nature and an impulse to take up a hammer and saw at any sight of lumber. This collision hatched custom display racks complete with wares that wobbled their way out of the Jungle Patch and into Kauai boutiques.

My first greeting cards were actually not cards at all. They were jacket covers for DVD amateur action films I edited from our family videos. As my Photoshop skills grew, I experimented making Kauai scenery collages paired with inspirational captions and fitted into rustic frames made in my jungle woodshop. These flopped in consignment test markets. Seeing my frown, Sharon suggested, "Why not turn your collages into greeting cards?" A light turned on.

My first cards were handmade folded cardstock blanks with 4x6 prints attached and sealed in clear display bags. I also made fridge magnets—wallet-sized versions of the cards inserted into acrylic magnetic mini frames. The monotony of cutting, folding, peeling double stick tape, and stuffing envelopes to make an inventory was brightened by working with the kids while binge-watching Netflix.

Armed with an inventory, I set out to get my product into seven stores—the same number of display racks I had made out of mahogany plywood saved from garage door shipping crates. Their theme was plantation Hawaii: a simple box, four feet high and eleven inches on each side, painted in light green ("oops" paint from Home Depot). Contrasting hunter green card holders lined each side. On the top was a miniature red roof. Borrowing from garage door physics, I installed salvaged bearing sets and torsion shafts set in x-shaped wooden bases which allowed the racks to spin flawlessly.

Convincing the merchants to budget some floor space for a rack was only half the battle. The issue now was whether or not customers would shell out five bucks to buy a card or magnet. It was a tricky cat-and-mouse game impacted by many whims: weather, luggage space, and even rack location within the store. In the fledgling days, I was losing the game. Soldiering on, I designed new cards hoping to find the exact ones tourists would buy. Each design took hours and sometimes days to make. It was disheartening when they didn't sell. There were times when I thought to cut my losses and throw in the towel.

Coming to the rescue were two game-changing designs. Using a random rooster photo taken on a family picnic, I added a Happy Father's Day caption. A band of fluffy chicks with their mother supplied a kicky Happy Mother's Day meme. Both designs sold out instantly. This gave me the vision that Kauai tourists were gaga for chicken souvenirs.

I began to crank out Rooster Humor occasion cards as fast as my brain could dream them up. There were roosters howling at the moon and mug shots of roosters slapped on a wanted poster. There were chickens surfing, golfing, and even getting married. On the back of each card a folksy explanation unraveled the mystery of Kauai's teeming wild poultry. (The short version: no predatory mongoose here.)

As card quality increased, so did sales. I eventually got my cards into thirty shops including the Newsstand at the airport. Production efficiency improved when I found a local print shop to print the cards (good bye double-stick tape) and

Rooster Humor rack

a mainland company that produced single metal-faced magnets. I now had some breathing room to begin T-shirt and hat designs. Last of all, I tweaked the rack design by making additional racks with a chicken wire motif. Atop the red roof was the company logo: a yellow pedestrian sign with the silhouette of a strutting rooster.

Of all the rewards that came from building Rooster Humor, the one I treasured most was

Bestseller card

adding a smile to someone's day. One morning while restocking product at a shop, I stepped back a pace to watch a senior couple perusing the cards and chortling. Of course I was happy when they bought a card, but I was even more happy knowing Rooster Humor had done its job.

THE TOUGHEST CLOSE: KIDS UNDERSTANDING FINANCES

Although not excelling in career acumen, one thing I am fairly good at is managing what money I have (thank you, dear Mother). Both before and during Kauai, Sharon and I followed the "pay as you go" budget plan. Having few material assets in our early years of marriage, we employed a gut-check: "So this (fill in the blank) would be perfectly awesome to have, but can we live without it?" This simple phrase fortified us to resist the lure of impulse buying and falling for wants beyond our reach. On holidays and birthdays we sometimes splurged a bit for the kids but never beyond our means. This made special occasions special. Furthermore, credit cards were eyed as a wolf in sheep's clothing. We learned to pay them off monthly and use them as a tool to earn airline miles.

THE FRUGAL BUZZER

There were times when I may have taken frugality a bit far—like the day I invested $20 in a hair clipper. "You can either have a bowl cut or a single-length buzz for free. For more finesse, go see your barber," I announced, "but plan on using your own spending money. Females are excluded." I figured this would save us about $60 per month. At first my haircuts were okay with the kids. Sharon and I thought they looked handsome prancing around with buzzed heads. Then their hormones hit.

"Don't touch my hair," Isaac said one day. "I'm off to Aunty Lisa's for a cut, and I'm mowing her lawn in exchange."

"Fine with me," I smiled.

Eric and Lucas outsourced to Lisa as well—until they hit an I-don't-need-my-hair-cut phase. This did save them money, but made for two primeval hairstyles, nicknamed wolf and poodle hair, respectively.

THE MONEY TREE AND FISHING

All parents have a tough job in teaching kids about finances. In my opinion, parents can do the easy thing—make nice and buy, buy, buy for their kids. Or they can be enough of a Scrooge to help them become as self-reliant as possible. In the case of the latter, parents find themselves walking a tight-rope. They must expertly sense the precise timing when a child has matured enough so as to avoid freaking them out when they break the horrid news, "My dearest children, alas, money doesn't grow on trees."

To soften our hard-nosed image, Sharon and I taught from the old Chinese proverb, "If you give a man a fish, you feed him for a day; if you teach him how to fish, you feed him for a lifetime." This helped us look a little more like wise sages than preachy parents.

To help us teach fishing we networked with business own-ers in the community. Roger, our attorney friend, hired the children to clean his office, paint his house, do his yard work, and organize his garage sales. More trusted jobs included scanning legal documents and running errands for his office staff. The children were also hired by Greg, a plain-spoken, hard-driving businessman with a big heart. He owned Har-bor Mall, a retail and restaurant cluster, handily situated down the road from our house. At Harbor Mall, the kids washed trolleys, tended to the grounds, manned the parking booth, worked shifts for shop owners, and helped patch the mall's roof.

Working for Greg had its surprises.

"Andy," Greg yelled as he got out of his truck.

"What's up," I tossed back, running out the door.

I saw Jordan bailing out of the truck, holding a bloody towel on his head and looking a little stunned. Greg blurted out, "Dude, Jordan got cut by a metal shelf that tipped over. You can take him to the hospital to get stitched, or I've got some super glue in the glovebox and we can glue him shut." Really, was he serious? I politely declined his battlefield medic services and took Jordan in for a proper stitching up.

THE GOLF BALL BUSINESS

Aside from working for business owners, the kids became apprentice business owners themselves when they opened a second-chance golf ball store. It all began by accident on a morning hike below some ocean cliffs at the nearby golf course. I heard hollering from the bushes.

"Geez, look at all the golf balls! Dad, can we keep them?"

"Well, we should probably be Good Samaritans and clean up the trail," I conceded.

Filling their pockets on this hike, and on many hikes after, resulted in a stockpile of four thousand plus stray balls. My, oh my . . . what were we to do with all those orphaned little white spheres that now filled every bucket and container we owned? We could either repatriate them to the cliff bottoms, take up golfing ourselves, donate them to the thrift shop, or set up a roadside pro shop. We decided on the latter, which produced two far-reaching benefits for the kids, one expected and one unexpected.

The expected benefit was that they learned some basics of commerce: product advertising, procurement, preparation, and display. And lastly, there was accounts receivable (their favorite). Up went a big white wooden sign at the top of our lane. (Directly across the road happened to be a world-class golf course.) It enticed, "Golf Balls 25 cents and up."

Weekly hunts restocked inventory. "Look, I found three PRO-V1's," Lucas gloated.

"My backpack is full," groaned Aaron. "Time to go!"

"Not yet," Lucas retorted, "I know there're more in that clump of bushes over there."

The collected inventory was then dumped into a sudsy metal wash tub. No kid was too young to scrub a golf ball. "Look at all these logo balls," smiled Isaac as he scrubbed a ball with a well-known U.S. President's face on it. (This along with other unique balls went into the collectables bin.)

The older kids then sorted the gleaming balls by condition and quality into glass-faced wooden bins located under the carport. The prices were painted on each bin in calligraphy, compliments of Isaac: 2 for 25 cents (for the shabby ones) all the way up to $2.00 for the high-end labels.

Then came the wait. The noise of car doors opening in

Lucas procuring merchandise

Aaron performing quality assurance duties

the driveway signaled customers. Muffled conversation was accompanied by the sound of rattling as customers sorted through the bins. When the rattling had stopped and the car doors had closed came a moment of great suspense—did they buy any balls? Katherine was usually the first to peel out the door to check the self-serve cash box. Often inside was a har-

First finds sorted

Jungle Patch Pro Shop

vest of quarters or dollar bills. Hurrah! 100% return on our investment!

At times the customers knocked on the door. I sent the kids out to meet and service them—leading to an unexpected bonus. Following our big white-and-green sign, golfers from all over the world wandered down into the Jungle Patch. They hailed from the Mainland, Canada, Australia, Europe, Mexico, Japan, and Taiwan, and talked story with our merchant children. Who knew picking up a few golf balls on a hike below the cliffs would bring the world to our doorstep?

Managing the golf ball business and working for business owners certainly didn't make the kids rich, but it did expose them to the basics of making a living. It also gave them a bit of start money for their future. And perhaps best of all, it helped prepare them for the jolt of a future adult reality: money doesn't grow on trees.

KID COMMENTS

Isaac (13/30)

A quick bike ride away from the Jungle Patch was a popular golf course. Just off the edge of its well-manicured greens were ocean cliff bottoms where swatches of buffalo grass greedily swallowed many an errant tee shot. At first we were finding golf balls for the novelty of it. We especially enjoyed finding the ones with logos on them.

Dad quickly realized we could sell them for money, which took our finding efforts to a whole new level. If you ever want to experience finding money on the ground in large quantities look no further than the hills adjacent to the nearest golf course. Based on the brand and condition, each ball could fetch anywhere from twenty-five cents to two dollars. If you found the right place where the golf balls collected due to rain runoff, it was like finding a vein in a goldmine—jackpot!

Isaac (Personal Journal, age 16)

On Tuesday Isaac Stennett mowed Aunty Lisa's lawn to pay Lisa back for cutting his hair. It took a very long time and he was very tired afterwards. Then he and the rest of the Stennett family ate hamburgers for Aaron's cub scout pack meeting.

Isaac (School Essay, age 15)

A work experience I'd rather forget reminded me how I want to get an education so I can get a job I want. One day, Theresa Park called me and asked if I could work for her tomorrow. I said yes, but in my mind I was thinking of what a bad time it would be. The next day she picked me up, and we drove to the seaport (she owns a clothes store and we had to pick up a shipment of clothes). Back at her store, I took the pen she handed me, horror-struck at the arduous task that lay before me—marking all the tags. After those tags she pulled out more. Then some more. By the time she finally announced we were leaving I had carpal tunnel. I followed her to the car. She paid me some money and I went home. I didn't really care about the money. I can see clearer than ever before, how I want to work a good job, and an education will help me to do so.

Katherine (School Essay, age 12)

These past few months I have been going with J'net Wheable to help teach at Island School. I do this on Wednesdays and Thursdays. On Wednesdays I go at 2:30 p.m. and teach for a few hours then I go to orchestra for two hours, which I can't say is very fun. On Thursdays I go at 1:00 p.m. for my lesson at J'net's house. Then we leave to go to Island School. We end at about 5:00 p.m. I enjoy it, but I also get paid for doing it.

Jordan (2/19)

While at KCC, I had the opportunity to work in the tutoring center as a tutor for writing, science, and math. This gave me a good opportunity to meet many interesting people. In my view, if one could imagine the most chill, relaxed job ever, it still wouldn't compare with tutoring at KCC. You pretty much walk into the center, slip a name tag on, and wait for students to come up with homework problems. If the problems seemed too difficult you could simply refer the student to one of the more advanced tutors (though it was always nice when you were actually able to help someone out).

CHAPTER FOURTEEN

The Adventure of Making a Difference

Armed with hammer and crowbar, I am ripping out a stubborn meshed sheet of ceramic tile in the bathroom of the Ryan house in Kekaha. Installation of a handicap shower is to follow demolition. Lucas and Aaron are dragging the extracted tile sections outside the house for disposal. Isaac and Eric are helping other volunteers screw down new plywood subflooring. My sons and I have answered the call to help a family in need. Lonnie, the father, has lost his job as caretaker of an apartment complex. His wife, Maile, is a diabetic and has had multiple amputations to preserve her life. Her father had left her the one material thing he had: a neglected house on Hawaiian homelands. It was the best option for them. Joining a brigade of volunteers, we do a rushed makeover. We tune up the plumbing and the electrical. We install a handicap ramp and shower. We even paint the walls to brighten the lives of the Ryans who have fallen on hard times. Who knew that such needs exist in paradise?

It had been a spirited ride on the crest of a wave of serendipity. We had visited Kauai for a season in the sun and wound up living a life in the sun. In our Jungle Patch, we studied, we worked, we played, we laughed. Sounds like Utopia, right? Truthfully it was . . . and it wasn't.

There were times when living here made me feel like I was

Kauai—lovely and relaxing, but isolated

stranded on a rock in the middle of the deep blue sea. Island fever, as it is called, is not an uncommon syndrome for transplants—instigated by a sudden realization that Hawaii is the most isolated population center on Earth.

For me, island fever spiked in cycles often triggered by a nomad's claustrophobia of only 75 miles of highway and a yearning to be nearer to our aging parents. There was also my lingering worry that I had hindered my family by not permanently settling down. Each April I thought of the beautiful spring unfolding in Idaho with spunky kid goats frolicking on green pastures. I reasoned that it wasn't too late. We could easily move back and, as a family, build Sharon's log home. The floors would be level, the roof leak-free, and there would be no more battle of the bugs!

Another trigger was island economics. Our financial road in Hawaii had been rocky. One of the biggest rocks was a large investment that went south. I had naively invested about one-third of our fixer-upper home profits with a charismatic, older businessman—a trusted friend. He guaranteed hefty returns, which showed up at first, but later dried up when the Ponzi scheme he had been sucked into got busted. This was a staggering blow. (I know you told me so Mamma: if it's too good to be true, it is.)

Another rock was Sharon's open heart surgery at Queen's Medical Center on Oahu to repair a congenital defect. Besides being a physical and psychological bombshell for Sharon (and a huge worry for me and the kids), it set us back financially for many months. A few years later, a nursing strike, lasting several months, dealt another financial blow.

LOGIC LOSES TO *KE AKUA*

Whenever my maroon fever spiked, I steeled myself in logic, mapped out a relocation plan with Sharon, and pledged to leave Hawaii. But there was always a force at play that melted my resolve. That force—exceeding even the lure of fine beaches and rollicking treks—was a unique adventure that presented itself to us: the opportunity to make a bit of a difference on the island.

Unseen behind the posh walls of Kauai's resorts are the faces of ordinary parents (like me) trying to make a living and hold their families together. Although most do fine, some hunch beneath the burden of putting bread on the table. Some even struggle to resist the lure of substance abuse to help them cope. Having been raised in a broken home, I am empathetic to the plight of struggling families. When I was age ten, my parents split in a bitter divorce, largely due to my father's abuse of alcohol. Lost and confused, I bounced back and forth between them, until I finally settled with my mother. Although I do have some good memories of my father, I remember growing up mostly without him.

I honestly don't fault either of my parents, and my stormy

family past actually had a silver lining: it forged a future goal within me to be a committed husband and an involved father. Now experiencing the joyful fulfillment of that goal (it's a continual work in progress), I want to pay it forward and help other families wherever possible. I believe that nothing can replace strong families as the foundation of stability and basic happiness for an individual, an island, a country—or a world.

I also believe that strengthening families can best be accomplished by having faith in *Ke Akua* or God. I acknowledge the various reasons to doubt the existence of *Ke Akua*— such as inexplicable tragedies. For me, I wonder, why would a merciful God allow my little brother and sister to pass away in their infancy? Tragedies notwithstanding, I fully believe our existence is not due to some cosmic accident. I'm not sure why I have such childlike faith. Maybe it's as some geneticists have claimed—that there's a specific gene that impels people to be spiritually minded. From that empirical viewpoint, I guess I must have gotten that gene. That said, I also believe such a gene can be cultivated.

For example, when I consider the impeccable order of numberless galaxies discovered by brilliant scientists, the faith gene within me grows. I have never seen anything organize itself, especially not in a family! Why would numberless galaxies in the universe be any different? It might sound cliche, but in my experience, where there is a design, there is always an equally intelligent designer. Furthermore, I have learned I am not as strong and independent as I'd like to think I am. Though I have prided myself on being a stand-your-ground farm boy, I have had to be rescued physically and emotionally throughout my life from things beyond my control.

Of these rescues, one in particular comes to mind. Before moving to Kauai, I was on a father-son work outing with Isaac and Eric. We were driving in our one-ton truck from St.

Charles to Utah, towing a twenty-foot flatbed trailer loaded with 10,000 pounds of baled hay strapped tightly down. The hay was proud produce from our farm, which we were going to sell to horse owners in Salt Lake County. We had crested Parley's Summit near Park City and began the steep, curving descent on Interstate 80.

As the truck picked up speed, I had the sinking realization that the electric trailer brakes were not working, and I had only the truck brakes to slow our hurtling load down and keep us on the road. Even if I could have somehow downshifted the manual transmission, the extreme rpms would have likely blown the motor. As we sped into the steep curves of Parley's Canyon, the trailer began to sway uncontrollably and threatened to tip over. If it did, the trailer's safety chains attached to the truck would drag us with it. Speeding traffic was present on all sides. I feathered the truck brakes all I could to avoid overheating them and causing their complete failure. I looked at my unknowing, trusting little sons and felt helpless to keep them and surrounding motorists safe. That's when I did the sensible thing I had always done on the farm as a boy: I uttered a silent prayer to my Maker.

My prayer was answered. On a flatter stretch of road, my panic was eased, and I had the presence of mind to somehow get the truck and trailer under control and slowed down enough to gear down. From there, we made it safely out of the canyon. It may sound dramatic to some, but I have had many such prayers answered in my life. Though they are not always answered as quickly and in the way I want them to be answered, they are always eventually answered.

WHY I SAID YES

Because of experiences like these—and because of my desire to help strengthen other families—at the eight-month mark of our sojourn, I accepted the surprising invitation to serve as a bishop (non-paid minister) for a Mormon ward (congregation) on Kauai. Although I knew this was the chance of a lifetime to meet numerous other families and help promote stronger family ties, at first, I balked. "Uhh . . . sounds exciting, but can I get back to you in a day or two?" I fumbled out to the church official who invited me.

Although my spiritual heart was saying yes, my temporal head was grumbling no. The carefree mood of our continuing season in the sun would definitely take a hit. Serving as a bishop for a period of five to eight years in the Church of Jesus Christ of Latter-day Saints (the official name of the Mormon church) makes no temporal sense at all! It's like working a part-time job and being on-call 24/7 for free, with zero financial benefits—zilch, nada, none.

Sharon and I decided that I should take a solo trip back to Idaho for a few weeks to put some affairs in order and process the dominoes that would fall if I accepted this assignment. While meandering across our Bear Lake farm, I envisioned my kids and me fitting together the stout timbers that would become Sharon's log home. Remembering this fond dream seemed to be my answer that we should keep our calendar free of long-term Kauai commitments.

But then, I began to reflect on the golden experience we had had during our first Sunday worship in the Lihue Ward. As we walked into the chapel, we were caressed by radiant sunlight and trade breezes streaming through the jalousies. Even more radiant were the smiles of the locals who greeted us.

One beaming *kane*, Alika Kelekoma, shook my hand,

and asked, "How are you, handsome?" Feeling pretty good about myself, I wound up to reply, whereupon he interrupted, "There I go, talking to myself again." I loved it!

At the end of the service we were invited to stand at the front of the chapel, along with the two dozen or so other visitors. Then the locals rose up and sang to us "Aloha Oe," accompanied by the pleasing drone of the organ. Vibrating through the choir of voices were the soothing base tones of Alika Kelekoma. Smiling local aunties placed a yarn lei—knitted by them—around the neck of each visitor. Tears streamed down my face—although I refused to admit it, I somehow knew we would be sharing friendships with these lovely people for a very long time. Recalling this exalted moment gave me my answer. I now knew that I had unfinished business on Kauai.

"Sharon," I said upon returning, "I'm going to accept the call. I want to make a difference for Kauai's families as much as I possibly can."

She smiled and nodded, "I know, it will work out."

ROUND ONE

I was grateful for her unflinching support, but I was unsure about how the kids would react. I found out when I came home in the afternoon on my first Sunday as bishop.

"Hey look, it's Bishop Stennett," they laughed and teased.

"Ha ha, it's cool you're the bishop, Daddy."

This sounded reassuring, but I wondered what they were really thinking. Is Dad going to have any free time for us now? And since they knew all my faults, maybe they were puzzled how their imperfect dad could be a minister for *Ke Akua*. I knew that the best way to sooth these concerns was to make this ministry a family adventure. I resolved then to take them with me, whenever possible, into the trenches of making a difference.

Round one was involving the older kids as speakers in sacrament meeting (worship service).

"Hey, Isaac, we need a youth speaker next week, can you talk on gratitude?"

"Daaaad," he replied, "are we going to have to speak every week?"

"No, and I know you'll do a great job."

Sharon also spoke occasionally, but her regular Sunday "job" was teaching a class of five and six-year-old children. She often asked, "How do you handle the responsibility of being a bishop for 600 people?"

I replied with a question of my own, "How do you handle teaching a class of six-year-olds every Sunday?" How she did that for nine years, I'll never know!

Inviting people to our home was an easy way to involve the family in service. "Dad, Mom said the Luders are coming to dinner today," exclaimed Katherine as I stepped through the door after another Sunday afternoon of interviews. Sharon usually invited someone over for a Sunday evening meal, and Katherine was eager to help. She especially liked playing her violin for a more appreciative audience than her brothers. Katherine's enthusiasm and the aroma of a roast beef dinner put some fuel back in my tank. "Oh, the Luders," I said. "They are new to the island. That's good, we want to make them feel welcome." Sharon had all hands on deck as the kids scurried around—setting the table, pouring the water, and mashing the potatoes (Aaron's specialty). After dinner, we all moved to the living room to talk story, and enjoy violin and piano concerts. For seventeen years our jungle house kitchen hosted people from every profession and walk of life. The only pecking order in the Jungle Patch was outside among the wild chickens.

HOME VISIT SPOOFS

We loved to have people in our home, but we also wanted to visit people in their own homes. I always reserved one special evening per week to hit the road and be with the people. Among the children I took as my wingman, Lucas held the record for attracting the most spoofs. On a visit to the Tovi house, Tevita, an elderly Tongan man, and his wife, Collette, greeted us at the door.

"Hi, Uncle, hi Aunty," Lucas said as he sunk into their soft couch.

"Lucas, can you please share our inspirational message tonight?" I asked.

"Well, um . . . we should all love one another," he began. His message was short and sweet, but got the point across. I then talked story for a while. Though in his late seventies, Tevita still worked hard physical labor building rock walls for a living.

"Tevita, how's your day been?" I asked.

"Build da rock wall. HOT." he replied in his Tongan English.

"You must be tired?"

"Mmm, like da boy." His amused eyes fell on Lucas. "Stay seeping." Sure enough, by this time, Lucas was fast asleep on their couch.

On a visit to the Sa family, Lucas was invited to say a prayer. I thought it was going well until he ended it with, "And please bless this house that no pestilence will come upon it, amen." Scriptorian Sister Sa looked at him a little strangely, and I wondered if the pest wars of the Jungle Patch were getting to him.

Lucas also seemed to be a magnet for improbable timing. We were in an apartment complex searching for a church member who we heard might be on the edgy side. Knocking on his screen door we heard a loud command inside, "Get the [expletive] out of here." Frightened Lucas beat a swift retreat down the sidewalk. I was shocked, too, until I deduced it was merely dialogue from the TV inside the apartment.

FRIENDSHIPS WITH THE *KUPUNA*

Of all of the friendships we gained through our ministering, the ones I treasured most were with the *kupuna*. *Kupuna* in Hawaiian means an elderly person, but it conveys a much deeper concept. It is a title honoring their wisdom gained by passing the crucible of life.

Some of my most favorite visits were to the homes of two widowed *kupuna* sisters, Mary and Connie. Their bloodline traced back to the royal family lines of Kauai. On a visit with Aaron to Mary's house, I noticed through the open door of a small side room thick stacks of what resembled memory albums.

Mary volunteered, "That room is my genealogy room, where my entire family tree is recorded. It took me decades to put together." Aaron sat perfectly still, knowing Aunty Mary was all about law and order. (As church librarian, she ensured no one checked out a piece of chalk without promising their right arm as collateral.)

As the visit wound down, Mary fetched a fresh loaf of her famous Portuguese sweet bread, and gave it to Aaron. He broke into a huge smile, "Thank you, Aunty." She made dozens of loaves by hand every day. Sometimes she made house calls. Down the Jungle Patch lane she would venture in her faith-powered jalopy.

"Look," Katherine cried, "It's Aunty Mary, and I'll bet she is bringing us some bread."

Kupunas Alika, Arde, and Mary

I smiled knowing my spaghetti dinner would be that much better. Her passing in 2004 brought sorrow to all. Of course we would miss her sweet bread, but we would especially miss her sweet example of a blameless, selfless life.

Mary's younger sister was Connie (aka Aunty Spike). I took Isaac along on one of my visits to her house. She was experiencing some health concerns. I asked, "Aunty, has the doctor figured out what's ailing you?"

She replied, "Hah, he said I've had too many birthdays, that's all!" Chuckling, I asked her to recite a favorite scripture verse or two. She obliged.

"Connie, thank you. I'm told that you used to teach the early morning seminary class for our teenagers—for many years. How did you manage it all?" That's when she opened up about her past.

"Bishop, a long time ago, I used to go out and drink with the girls all night. It was hard to admit that I couldn't stay sober."

"I wouldn't have ever guessed," I interjected.

Kupuna Connie

"I know, but then one day I realized it was wrong—what I was doing to my family. That's when I turned to *Ke Akua*. I've been sober for decades." She excused herself from the room and returned carrying a sack of goodies. Isaac suddenly perked up. "Here, Isaac, take these home to your brothers and sister."

"Thanks, Aunty."

I left that night resolving that when I grew up, I wanted to be as humble, kind, and honest as *kupuna* Connie.

AN UNSUNG GREATEST LOVE STORY

Among all the examples of selflessness we witnessed on Kauai (and perhaps anywhere), none was more inspiring than that of *kupuna* Arde Yamashita. Her dedication to her husband, George, was one of the great love stories of all time. In his early years, George had been a robust surfer guy. When I met him, he was paralyzed from the neck down due to a diving accident. Because she loved him so much, Arde married George, not before, but after his accident. Over the years, each of our children and I had many opportunities to visit George and Arde.

"*Howzit,* Brother George?" I would begin.

He would smile and usually say, "No complaints, Bishop. Man, that breeze feels nice."

George loved music. "Did Katherine bring her violin?"

"Yup, sure did."

George would then close his eyes and smile as music filled the room. Katherine's face glowed as her notes produced a broad smile on his lips.

I could scarcely imagine what emotional demons he must be battling, trapped in a motionless body.

"Bishop, I was wondering if you could give me a blessing."

"My pleasure, Brother George."

I then laid my hands on his head. After the amen, he spoke with glowing eyes of his one getaway in life, "Sitting at the beach in the warm sun and watching the waves roll in . . . I could do that forever."

Meanwhile, Arde sat quietly. I knew changing bedpans and dressings for fourteen years had exacted its toll, but she never complained. When George's soul slipped away, I sought to comfort her, "Arde, I can see George now, waiting for you with a prime seat on *Ke Akua's* eternal beach, watching the waves roll in. Your love story has only begun."

DRYING TEARS

Aside from a full day of Sunday routines and weeknight visits, I was on call 24/7. Although I involved the family as much as possible, when the phone rang and confidences needed to be kept, I had to go it alone. I never minded answering a call; it meant an opportunity to make a difference for a struggler. Sometimes a phone pep talk did the trick, but other times a face-to-face visit was needed. I did my best to be a sounding board and help them connect with *Ke Akua's* grace.

Some of the most wrenching visits were with individuals suffering clinical depression or mental instability. I realized they needed more than my spiritual counseling. I did my best to connect them with professional services, but I often felt helpless to relieve their suffering. If nothing else, they knew there was at least one person in the world that cared about them. In all my ministering, I learned an empathy that forbade me to judge. Lurking below the surface of dysfunction are issues that others cannot fathom unless they have walked a mile in that person's shoes.

Unexpected deaths were by far the most difficult calls to handle—especially when it was a tourist that passed away. In one such case, a retired gentleman had come to Kauai working on his dream quest to see the world's wonders when a massive stroke left him unconscious in the ICU. I was called to offer him a blessing of healing. As I laid my hands on his head and gave him the blessing, I sensed it was his time to depart. Soon thereafter, he did.

His daughter flew in from the mainland to settle his affairs. Because of his health risk history, he had told her that wherever he wandered in his travels (a kindred spirit of mine), if he were to pass, that's where he wished to be buried. To honor his wish, his daughter and I held a graveside memorial service. Joined by Alika Kelekoma, I read words from the Book of Revelation: "They shall hunger no more, neither thirst anymore; neither shall the sun light on them, nor any heat. For the Lamb which is in the midst of the throne shall feed them, and shall lead them unto living fountains of waters: and God shall wipe away all tears from their eyes."

After Alika had dedicated the grave and we had sung, "Till We Meet Again," we embraced his daughter who was both teary-eyed and smiling. I felt confident we had supported her in fulfilling her father's wishes to be buried in the final stop of his dream quest, the heavenly Garden Isle, thus giving her a foothold of closure.

TYING KNOTS

Ministering to people wasn't only helping them through the sad moments of life. There were the light-hearted moments as well—like performing wedding ceremonies. Many couples were from the mainland. Surprisingly, their requests were often last minute. I never minded though, and happily showed up to the many oddball venues they had chosen to be married in.

One couple wanted to stand on beachside boulders while the water swirled around us. One bride fainted into the arms of her fiance. (Was it due to nerves or awe at my perky sermon?) Another couple wanted to hold the ceremony as close as possible to the surf's edge with their backs to the ocean, facing me on the upside of the beach. The bride was wearing, yes, a frilly white wedding gown with a train, and the groom, a tux. I sensed a blooper about to happen (never turn your back to the ocean, right?). But not wanting to seem bossy, I said nothing. Sure enough, as I was offering yet another perky wedding sermon, a mischievous wave soaked the lower quarter of the bride and groom. I paused for an awkward moment. "Everything okay?" I asked. To my relief they laughed it off, and I finished the ceremony with no more maritime interruptions.

WHAT'S DAD DOING HERE?

Such were the routines and adventures my family and I had while I served as a Mormon bishop on Kauai. Before I knew it, seven and a half years had flown by, and I was formally released from my bishop's duties in a Sunday worship service. Afterwards, I boxed up the few personal effects I had in my office, held a conference with the newly-called bishop, and handed him the building keys. Then I drifted home uncustomarily early to my family that afternoon.

A little lost and with extra time on my hands, I began to process my family's many years of caring for souls. I realized that my ordinary family and I had been beyond lucky to be part of an extraordinary life-changing journey. Our goal had been to make a difference for Kauai families, but being inside their circles, we had been transformed by their goodness into better human beings ourselves.

Not long after my release, I was invited to perform additional ministering duties (helping look after all six of Kauai's congregations for another nine years). I got to be friends with a widening circle of remarkable people, ranging from hula gurus to taro farmers to a rodeo cowboy turned gospel preacher.

In learning from our Kauai friends, there were two qualities I wanted to emulate the most. First was the spirit of aloha—barrier-free giving, gentleness, and openness. Second was their keen sensitivity to divinity. For so many Polynesians, the veil between the material world and the eternities is thin.

One testament of this is a prophetic statement uttered to me by a *kupuna* Tongan prior to our departure to Kauai. Fritz Wolfgang worked in the family business of Jet's Airfreight in Salt Lake City, Utah. As he helped our family load our few household belongings into a shipping crate, he asked, "Where are you going?"

I responded, "Oh, we're gonna go hang out in Kauai for a few months."

Moments later, he looked me in the eye, and flatly stated, "You will be there a very long time."

I had never met him before, nor have I seen him since—and I was shy to ask what he meant. But now after seventeen years of laboring to serve Ke Akua's children and families on Kauai, I understand what he meant and where he got that prophetic note for me.

KID COMMENTS

Isaac (13/30)

Kauai has an Adopt-a-Highway program to keep the highways clean. Four times a year we would wake up early Saturday morning and walk down King Kaumualii highway picking up litter. Waking up early on Saturday made me wish we had not adopted a highway; but service opportunities like these helped me realize that other people exist besides myself, and that happiness comes from helping others.

Thursday night meant visiting lots of people from the local congregation. We'd gather in my Dad's small office to get our visiting partner and list of people to visit. You never knew quite what to expect as you knocked on a stranger's

Isaac and Eric join friends Kara and Rudy for adopt-a-highway

door. Most of the time it was a smile but sometimes you'd get an angry dog or person. Visiting all these people through the years helped me cultivate empathy and respect for people from all walks of life.

Lucas (School Essay, age 14)

Thursdays and Sundays are a little different. Thursdays are pretty much the same as Tuesdays except for the fact that at 6:30 me and my older two brothers and my dad head out to the church to meet with other brethren of our church to go home teaching. Home teaching is pretty much just going out in pairs and visiting the members of our ward. We arrive home sometime around 9:00.

Sundays are the day when my whole family, except my dad because he's the bishop and has meetings to attend to, wakes up at somewhere around 8:00 and get ready for church. We leave at 8:30 and go to our different classes. Church starts at 9:00, and the first thing me and my two older brothers and I have is priesthood. Then we have Sunday school, and last is sacrament meeting. At around 12:00 we all arrive home. Well, my dad stays at the church to go to meetings and appointments cause you know he's bishop. I still don't know how he endures it all. Well, anyways we get home and just do mellow things the rest of the day.

Katherine (4/21)

I never jumped up when my dad invited me to go visit people with him, and I never went to an Adopt-a-Highway without slipping in a few complaints. I was wholly in it for the ice cream sundaes Dad was happy to provide afterwards. I used to wonder why serving others made him so happy. It was like the visits in themselves were ice cream sundaes to him. "Katie, bring your violin along," he would say. (I would roll my eyes a little, but was secretly excited to play for any audience that wasn't my brothers.) There was the gentle senior couple who loved the theme from *Romeo and Juliet* and the pensive gentleman in the rest home who loved Bach. As a 19-year-old missionary walking the streets of Louisiana years later, I was glad I had had those experiences with my dad. I toted my violin around and played Adele for the kids playing Four Square on the sidewalk. "Know any rap songs?" they asked. Didn't get those kinds of requests in nursing homes! One time we visited a lady named Rho. Though she didn't seem thrilled to see us, she invited us in. As we sat on the floor, I played for her. Her saddened face lit up immediately and, in that moment, I got it. This tasted way better than an ice cream sundae!

Aaron and Katherine prepare aloha mango delivery

An Empty Jungle Patch Nest

The kids have all left the Jungle Patch and Hawaii now, pursuing college, work, marriage, and their own adventures. Huzzah! That was our goal all along. But their flying solo signals the end of our odyssey. It also means Sharon and I are a vast ocean and long plane rides apart from them. And this once noisy jungle house—full of laughter and sometimes tears, video game hoopla, birthdays, holidays, Legos, King Arthur wooden swords, homeschool, friendships, and sometimes quarrels—is now horribly quiet.

Even the Jungle Patch itself is disappearing. Development is encroaching. The verdant jungle on the hillside hiding us from the highway has been stripped to the bare soil by chainsaws, men, and machines. Soon there are to be modern buildings I'm told. Outside the big picture window in the living room, the trampoline is still there. It was damaged by a fallen tree in the heavy rains and winds from a recent near-miss hurricane. I didn't have the heart to take it down. Inside our living room, still sitting on our shelves, are Jordan's sprawling Lego creations. He lovingly built them prior to departing for his church mission in Japan. We should probably take them down and put up a vase or something; but, again, we don't have the heart to do it.

I'm told the empty nest thing affects parents differently.

Some are glad, maybe even relieved of a burden when it happens. I am, of course, thrilled the children have sprouted wings to fly. Even so, when the last one left, I couldn't help but privately break down and weep. I felt my inner fortress of farm-boy grit tumbling before this daunting tremor of life. Thankfully, Sharon is a patient listener. I also go on daily "processing" bike rides round and round the golf course. Loneliness for the kids and the innocent Jungle Patch years still hits me now and again like the rogue wave that pummeled young Lucas on our first day at the beach. But I'm learning to hold my own.

From all my years of being a dad and being a husband to Sharon, I have gleaned volumes of perspective about true joy and lasting fulfillment. Is it found in career accomplishment, in amassing material comfort, in embellishing and perpetuating our physical looks? For me, at least, the answers to these questions can be condensed into a Jungle Patch proverb that came to me long ago: "One hundred years of selfish pleasure cannot equal even a single moment of family joy."

Though family joy is automatically connected with personal sacrifices and even sorrow at times (like when your children vacate the nest), I stand by the truth of that proverb.

Sharon and I have talked at length about what to do next. Should we finally pronounce an amen to our season in the sun? Should we become conventional again and move back to the sturdy brick home we kept on the mainland? (It has level floors, a roomy kitchen with cupboards, and no pests.) We've even considered a sequel season for the two of us in Thailand where my friend, Wichai, runs a ropes course with smiling Thai people in a quiet patch of forest outside of Bangkok. (That sounds outrageously gypsy and fun!) So far, we are still waiting to see where this will go.

Sometimes it seems inconceivable we could ever leave this

paradise. I shudder to think of not seeing our adopted Kauai *ohana*—our community and church friends. And how could I ever part with the relaxing culture of aloha where drivers yield their right-of-way to shaka-throwing sideroad traffic? And how could I ever subsist without a daily dose of Kauai scenery, which only grows more breathtaking by the day. I still have to almost pinch myself to make sure I'm not dreaming when I ascend to Kokee to do my Rooster Humor route, or do a bike ride to the lighthouse, or hike up Sleeping Giant with an island newcomer. Her gorgeous scenery is never commonplace to these eyes. Last of all, what about my friends, each golden beam from the lemon-yellow Hawaiian sun? As they light on my skin, they radiate peace to my soul and draw a contented smile upon my lips. They symbolize victory in my quest to gain respite from the snow trenches of Bear Lake. How could I ever survive without them?

These questions remain to be answered, but there are two questions I can answer for certain. Did I ever make peace with myself about breaking my resolution to quit my gypsy ways, and thus give stability to the family? In a benevolent twist of irony, following my tempting daydream to Kauai became the very means of keeping that resolution. Seventeen years in one place is the longest on record for me (birth to present) and the kids never had to change schools! And what about my country-boy dream of building Sharon a log home and raising young 'uns on our Bear Lake farm? Although some dreams die hard, Sharon and I are okay with it. We feel we made a fair trade in gaining seventeen years of family memories in a jungle house with a rusting metal roof, shaded by a jagged halo of Java plum and mango trees.

And so, for now, my season in the sun on Kauai will go on.

A Jungle Patch Husband

I first met Sharon in the sweltering heat and commotion of Bangkok, Thailand in 1982. We were both serving volunteer missions for the Church of Jesus Christ of Latter-Day Saints. She had recently begun her eighteen-month assignment, and I was nearing the completion of my two-year assignment. I was twenty-one and she was twenty-three. She was a charmingly cheerful and kind soul who lifted others with her bright smile amidst adversity and triumph. She had recently graduated from nursing school, had a good job, and a bright future ahead. But she decided it was time to give back to humanity and came to Thailand to chip in.

I think I first noticed her as she was giving typhoid booster shots to the hundred or so *farang* (non-Thai) missionaries in our mission (that was part of her assignment). I also noticed with admiration as she toughed out a five-month assignment with seven other missionaries to serve refugees in a UN camp in Phanat Nikhom. Even amongst the sweat, grit and grime of camp service, her cheerfulness never wilted. Of course, Mormon missionaries have a strict protocol to not date or fraternize while on their volunteer assignment. But imagine my delight when, after our missions, I had a purely by-chance meeting with her at a mutual friend's house in Salt Lake City, Utah.

I nervously asked, "Hey, do you want to come visit my

mom's farm in Idaho sometime?" I was pleasantly surprised when she smiled and said, "Yeah, that sounds fun!"

I preserved a delightful mental reel of highlights from the weekend of her visit: a pretty, bemused city girl in alien territory getting my tractor stuck in a ditch, riding a horse, and going to the cattle auction to watch cowboys and my mother buy cattle.

I knew a gem when I saw one, so in two months time I proposed. At a romantic vantage point in Utah, where I was attending college, I rallied all my courage. "Will you . . . hahahaha!" I was nervous and busted up laughing. I tried again. "Sharon, will you . . . hahaha!" Same result. Eventually, I got the question out, and, lucky for me, she said, "Yes!"

Country bumpkin that I am, I didn't know I was supposed to have a ring in hand to propose marriage. That came later when I took her ring shopping in Twin Falls, Idaho. Being a poor college student, I didn't have much cash so I blurted out to the jeweler (right in front of Sharon), "What do you have in the two-to-three-hundred-dollar range?"

"This one is $275."

Being a cattle jippo's son, I countered, "$200, final offer."

"$225, and it's yours, err . . . hers," she grinned and glanced at Sharon.

I nodded my okay. Boxing up the ring and handing me the receipt, she wished us well. I admit it was a tiny diamond, and the delivery was low on romance and certainly not worthy of the queen that Sharon is. But being the unassuming woman she is, Sharon donned it proudly on her finger on our wedding day. This frugality became the very symbol and methodology that has made our married lives so rich—not in material things, but in experiences.

Fast forward fifteen years later to Hawaii. I am sitting at Sharon's bedside at Queen's Medical Center in Honolulu. She has just undergone open-heart surgery to repair a congenital heart defect, discovered in a routine exam. She was asymptomatic, but was advised that she should have the hole between heart chambers repaired sooner rather than later. As I sit in her recovery room, seeing her hooked up to monitors and tubes, I am flummoxed at the pain she is going through and the sheer reversal of roles. She had always been the one at the family's bedside, compassionately massaging our pains, emptying barf pans, administering meds, and fetching cold glasses of water.

I am assured by the medical staff that she will recover fine, but there is always that anxious awareness of the thin veil existing between life and death. All that separates the two is a single heartbeat. That same feeling of anxious awareness filled my mind each of the six times she gave birth to our children. Would everything be okay with her and with our tiny, helpless infant being born? I am grateful in all these cases that she and our children remain at my side.

I don't suppose it is even possible to fathom the depths of devotion and selflessness required of a mother who gives

her all to her children. Their joy is her joy, their sorrow is her sorrow. To me, it's nothing short of living, breathing art that is so profoundly beautiful that it inspires its admirers to want to be kinder, gentler people. Better yet, it is a beacon of light illuminating the way for humankind to gain deliverance from life's gloomy corridors of me, me, me. At least it's been that way for me being married to Sharon.

Made in USA - North Chelmsford, MA
1043945_9780999730911
01.14.2020 1111